Rum, Bum and Concertina

George Melly

RUM, BUM AND CONCERTINA

WEIDENFELD AND NICOLSON LONDON

FOR MY MOTHER WITH LOVE,
AND IN MEMORY OF MY FATHER.

*Ashore it's wine women and song
Aboard it's rum bum and
concertina.*

Old Naval Saying

*Let the reader therefore understand
that the facts were what I say
they were, but the interpretation
that I give them is what I am —
now.*

Jean Genet *The Thief's Journal*

Chapter 1

I was sitting, less than a month off my eighteenth birthday, on the lavatory of the 'green bathroom' in my parents' large comfortable ugly house in the Victorian suburbs of Liverpool, and I was crying bitterly.

The reason I was crying was because I'd just read a letter from a man called A. B. Clifford who was a housemaster at Stowe, the school I'd just left, and, more relevantly in this context, Officer in Charge of the JTC there.

JTC stood for Junior Training Corps. When I'd arrived at Stowe, about a year after the beginning of the war, it was still called the OTC, but this had been changed to meet the democratic temper of the times. Officers Training Corps had suggested rather too blatantly that all public school boys were automatically officer material.

Changing an initial didn't mean changing anything else though. The ancient drill sergeant still called us 'sir', and we dressed up every Tuesday afternoon in 1914 uniforms with puttees and brass buttons. In the summer there were occasional 'field days' when we charged about the drowsy Buckinghamshire countryside pretending to shoot each other while perspiring 'umpires' decided whether we were 'dead' or not.

Playing these Henty-like games made it difficult at times to remember there was a real war on and that boys we'd known well had been killed in it. Like their more fortunate contemporaries most of them had done their initial training at either Oxford or Cambridge, an arrangement which assured them of a place after the duration if and when they returned. They'd usually come down during this academic interim looking carefully languid in their new Brigade of Guards' uniforms and, more often than not, enviably drunk. Then they'd be posted and a few months later we'd be told, in Chapel, that they'd been killed on active duty. A talented boy of Norwegian origin who liked to paint still-lives in the school art-school in what he called 'masturbational Pre-Raphaelite detail' was blown up in Africa. A debating society wit, as humane as he was clever, was mown down in Italy. Then, for a moment, we'd realize, with morbid but not unpleasurable intimations of mortality, that if the war went on long enough it might be our name that J. F. Roxburgh was reading out with a distinct and untypical tremor in the famous, much-imitated drawl.

Yet in my case, however much I might fantasize along these lines, I was enough of a realist to know that if I fell it wouldn't be in a commissioned uniform. I was patently not officer material. My puttees fell down, My buttons were either dull and smeary or, if halfway bright, the Duraglit had spread greasily over the surrounding khaki. Worse, I was always losing things and indeed, during the last week of my final term when the time had come to hand in my uniform, I'd discovered that I was short of a brass-buckled belt and one boot.

Thinking myself safe because I wasn't coming back, I'd concealed the loss from the retired sergeant in the 1820 gothic

armoury and left school in high spirits with several of my contemporaries; all of us defiantly puffing away at Black Balkan
Sobranies through the taxi window. My confidence was mis-
placed. The missing items were noted and reported to Major
Clifford. He bothered to write to me during his holidays, not
only demanding I paid for their replacement but warning me, in
an icy rage, that he intended writing to my future Commanding
Officer at the Navy Shore Establishment, Skegness, informing
him of my perfidious carelessness and suggesting some suitable
punitive action on my arrival there.

Unaware of what this might lead to, despite a brother and a
father currently in naval uniform, my notions of the Senior
Service were still coloured by the Charles Laughton version of
Mutiny on the Bounty; I wept and continued to weep until, as I'd
probably intended, my mother heard me and rattled the
Bakelite handle of the bathroom door to ask what was wrong.

Given that I was almost eighteen it may suggest a certain
emotional immaturity to cry quite so desperately for so slight a
cause, and the truth is that, while rather tiresomely sophisticated
in some directions, I was extremely undeveloped in others and
had, I would say now, an emotional age of about thirteen. Even
if Major Clifford had carried out his threat it was extremely
unlikely that a senior officer in command of the entire Royal
Navy intake during a major conflict at a particularly crucial
moment could have spared much time to work himself up over
the loss of two items of archaic military equipment at a distant
public school. Predictably, when I got to Skegness not a word
was said about either belt or boot.

My choice of the Navy is also indicative of my thinking during
that period. It had nothing to do with my younger brother's
success as a Dartmouth cadet nor my father's shore-based
commission in the RNVR. It was for no other reason than that I
found the uniform 'more amusing'.

Wearing plum-coloured corduroys and a pale pink shirt
(school uniform had been suspended at Stowe during the war),
I had explained this a month or two earlier to an outraged
Admiral in Cambridge. I'd been sent to see him by the school in

the hope that he might recommend me, like most of my contemporaries, for the year's training while attached to a college.
Enunciating with dangerous care, he told me he felt unable to do
so. Otherwise I had a pleasant day. I took an actress from the
local rep out to lunch – I'd met her through my mother when
she'd been at the Liverpool Playhouse. I went to visit some
pretty twins who painted identical whimsical pictures of cats
in a studio flat in Petit Curie – I'd a letter of introduction from
the couple who ran the Stowe art school. Then I'd gone back
and explained to J. F. Roxburgh, as sympathetic and ironic as
ever, that the Admiral and I hadn't really hit it off.

All in all then I was fairly confident that I would be wearing
my 'amusing' uniform for as long as the Navy chose to keep me.

The journey to Skegness, a meander across wartime Britain
involving a change of stations at Manchester, dragged on inter-
minably. On the second leg I shared a carriage with a robust
middle-aged Lancashire woman in a pixie-hood. She had two
children with her, a baby and a toddler whom she used as props
in a monologue aimed at demonstrating how rough yet warm-
hearted were her maternal feelings. The baby was changed twice,
with suitable comments on its copious stools. The little girl in
her pink cardy understandably whined a great deal and was
threatened or placated according to whim. At every step, and
there were many and all of uncertain duration, her mother, with
the single-minded insistence of a radio comic launching a new
catchphrase, yelled at her to 'gerraway fra' that door'.

I smiled at her occasionally in hypocritical if solicited endorse-
ment. At the same time I neutralized much of my irritation
by reminding myself that she was working class. My priggish if
emotional left-wing sympathies, springing in the main in reaction
to the Fascist sentiments of a hated prep-school headmaster,
automatically awarded good marks for humble social origin. The
fact was that I'd never met a member of the proletariat who
wasn't a nannie, tram conductor, plumber or school servant.

I was also in no position to criticize anyone for role-playing.
The book I was reading, Corvo's *Hadrian VII*, and the other

books I'd brought with me were as much to advertise my tastes to anyone who might share them as for their literary content. And so we sat there as the Lincolnshire landscape grew flatter in the heat, she playing mum, me sensitive aesthete, until at last, at about five-thirty in the afternoon, the train pulled into Skegness Station. I found the pass the Navy had sent me, and drifted towards the exit.

Although turned down for Cambridge I was still what was known as a 'Y scheme' rating; that was someone who was at least to be considered for a commission; a categorization based entirely on the fact that I'd been to a public school for, aside from my unfortunate brush with the Admiral, I'd no other contact with the Navy, taken no exam, attended no further interviews. Nor was there anything in my scholastic record to suggest a future officer. On the contrary I had managed to fail the elementary maths paper in my School Certificate and had made no attempt to take it again.

Even my having been accepted for the Navy at all was something of a privileged fiddle. Although entitled to state a preference, if you waited until you were called up you had no control over which of the services claimed you, and at that time, just before D-Day, it was more than likely to have been the Army. If however you were still at school you could volunteer for whatever branch you wanted at seventeen, thereby ensuring acceptance. Simultaneously you entered a plea to be allowed to finish your education; a ploy which almost automatically deferred your service until the time you'd have been called up anyway.

That was how I found myself rattling towards HMS *Royal Arthur* in a small Naval bus which was waiting outside the station for the new intake. I looked out at the almost deserted resort, the pier peeling, the rock and souvenir shops shut for the duration. Despite my tears of a month before, I wasn't in any way worried, simply curious.

What initially confused me about HMS *Royal Arthur* was the immediate sensation, later confirmed, of a certain architectural

5

frivolity completely inappropriate to a Royal Navy Shore Establishment. The rows of huts, the great concrete messes, the straight paths, even the formal flower beds, were explicable enough, but it was possible to see that, under the khaki or grey paint of the exterior of the buildings, were traces of shocking pink or baby blue, while the interior of the communal structures proved even stranger. On arrival, still in our civvies, we were marched to 'Collingwood Mess Block' for a meal. We queued up in a large lobby to draw our knives, forks and spoons through a hatch. The ceiling of the lobby was painted to represent a summer sky with fluffy white clouds passing across it. In the centre of the room, rooted in the bare floorboards, was a large and comparatively realistic tree. Part of the plaster from which it was constructed had fallen off to show a skeleton of wire-netting and metal scaffolding. The upper branches in no way tapered off, but terminated abruptly on contact with the painted sky. The serving hatch, through which a rather gloomy WREN galley rating passed us our eating irons, was framed by mullioned windows let into the elaborate façade of an Elizabethan inn with a sign reading 'Ye Olde Pigge & Whistle' projecting out over our heads. The dining hall itself made no effort to carry through this Merrie England ambiance, it was an exercise in whole-hearted if cut-price Odeon Art Deco. Our initial medical examination, on the other hand – 'Have you ever had a venereal disease? Bend over. Cough.' – took place in a plaster of Paris cave embedded with papier maché skeletons and treasure-chests.

As I soon discovered, HMS *Royal Arthur* had been built for another function. It was one of the first of Billy Butlin's holiday camps, all of which had been taken over by the Navy. Planned for the regimented pleasure of the Fairisle-jersied civilians of the late Thirties, they needed no more than a few coats of drab paint and a whaler on the swimming-bath to become wartime shore establishments. The redcoats were transformed into petty officers. The intercom system, through which the campers had been hi-de-hied to meals or jollied along to enter the knobbly knees competitions, now barked out our orders. The first morning, just to make quite sure we knew we were no longer subject to individual logic, we were made to get up at 5.30 a.m. As a public school-boy I was initially less thrown and unhappy than most of my working-class contemporaries. Being used to being away from home I was less homesick and despite Stowe's comparatively liberal approach to discipline, I found it that much easier to accept illogical orders. On the debit side I was less able to cope for myself. I lost more, looked grubbier and more untidy, and found it impossible to lay out my bedding and equipment with the required Mondrian-like precision. Luckily, however, I was an instinctive and practised tart and most of the Petty Officers were, platonically at any rate, easily seduceable.

Our Chief Petty Officer was a case in point. He looked rather like W. C. Fields and was quite old. Given his experience I suppose that he must have been near retiring age even by wartime standards or he would surely have been given a more taxing job than marching ninety young men around an intake camp. I fell for him because he combined a truly inventive obscenity with human sympathy; 'You're a fine specimen of hu-fucking-manity!' were the first words he spoke to me directly; and because, despite my patent inadequacies and determination to become a licensed jester, he quite clearly liked me.

Throughout the three and a half years I was to spend in the Navy I found that, in general, Petty Officers and Chief Petty Officers, if not religious maniacs or just nasty by nature, tended to be reasonable men. Long association with the sea and its ports had given them a certain tolerant sophistication, part cynical certainly but affectionately so. They had learnt to mistrust the moral imperatives of any one place because they had seen them replaced by others, often equally rigid and ridiculous, elsewhere. The made allowances too for us temporary sailors. We were there because we had to be. One day the war would be over and the Navy its old self: a machine for sailing in. The same attitude was common among regular ratings, especially those with long-service stripes. Many of them had been Petty Officers in fact but had been reduced to the ranks for some detected misdemeanour: habitual drunkenness, a too open penchant for young lads, jumping ship or failure of duty. They did, if very old, look a little absurd in bellbottoms but they were jolly fellows if in some cases a little pressing in their affections.

Warrant Officers on the other hand I could seldom abide. Martinets, sticklers for the letter of the law, hard resentful men who realized that they had risen from the ranks on merit but been blocked for a commission on class grounds. Caught uneasily between the relaxed bonhomie of the POs' mess and the easy formality of the wardroom they were punctilious in their insistence on outer form, correctitude, the marks of respect as laid down by King's Regulations. In particular the presence of public school-boys on the Lower Deck had a quite unsettling effect on them. Their perfectly understandable resentment at having to salute men much younger and less competent than themselves over the years tempted them to take it out on conscripts from the same social background as their 'superiors' yet, in fairness, their respect for the rules prevented them from yielding openly to the temptation to harass. It was just that if, as a middle-class rating, one erred, their reproaches or application of the primitive remedies available were delivered with a certain thin-lipped satisfaction not unlike that of a colour-prejudiced yet rigorously self-disciplined policeman happening upon an immigrant engaged in some provenly criminal act or a moderate anti-semite reading in a newspaper that a Jewish financier has been arrested for fraud. Retrospectively I can sympathize with those Warrant Officers but at the time, trapped myself in a web of confused class feelings, I teased them and yet resented it when they reacted as I'd intended.

With the Upper Deck it was easier. They behaved in general as if they were prefects and the middle-class conscript ratings were new boys. Occasionally, usually when slightly drunk on unaccustomed amounts of pink gin, some young sublieutenant would tell me, with an air of considerable condescension, that he'd known my brother at Dartmouth. There was also the odd officer, usually rather senior, who allowed himself to talk on a personal level to individual ratings. On the whole though contact with the Upper Deck remained minimal. Collectively we referred to them as 'the pigs', but except in the case of a particularly officious or unpopular officer, the epithet was dismissive rather than venomous.

The only officer obliged to remain in contact with the Lower Deck on an approachable basis was in fact the Chaplain. It was he who organized any extra-maritime activities like art shows or drama groups, and of course he was also responsible for our spiritual well-being. When I first joined the Navy I was still a vague believer in the existence of a personal God. After a great deal of hesitation and considerably later than most boys at Stowe, I'd been confirmed. (I have a suspicion that my doubts and eventual decision to accept communion were largely based on attracting additional attention.) I was aesthetically moved by the King James *Bible* and the *Book of Common Prayer*. I adored wallowing in the juicy harmonies of Victorian hymns, but the discovery that the Surrealists violently opposed Christianity had begun to shake my already pretty ramshackle faith, and the address to the new intake of ratings at *Royal Arthur* by the camp chaplain did little to prop it up. 'God', he told us in an inane parsonical bray, 'is the highest officer in the British Navy.'

Our Chief Petty Officer was a sceptic. On Sunday mornings he told us, 'You can crash your swedes until 08.30 hours, that is unless you wish to attend 'oly Commotion.'

Before our first Church Parade he told Roman Catholics to fall in at the front, and then asked if there were any Jews. There were two.

'Well, we 'aven't got no Rabbi,' he said, 'you'll 'ave to listen to the wireless,' and they were dismissed and told to stay in their chalets until the Highest Officer in the British Navy had been suitably piped aboard.

We were meant to be at 'Skeggy' for a fortnight before going on to another camp near Ipswich for further training. During this period we were marched about endlessly. 'Come on! Come on!' yelled our Chief when we were tardy at falling in. 'If you'd let go of yer cocks you'd get around a bloody sight quicker!' We had our urine analysed several times and were shown a film about the effects of VD – 'You're off to the pictures now to learn how to whip it in, whip it out and wipe it!' Due to the size of a screen designed for a full holiday-camp at the height of the season this proved a rather unnerving experience and several ratings fainted. I wasn't among them, but I did become hysterical with suppressed laughter while watching a silent documentary on the correct way to brush your teeth. The enormous lips opened to reveal teeth the size of important Victorian tomb-stones while a huge brush moved slowly up and down them, and a little later a King Kong-sized finger with a surprisingly dirty nail massaged the gigantic gums. We were looked at by psychia-trists to whom I swanked about my fondness for Eliot and Baroque architecture, but who all agreed with me instantly that I was sensible to favour the Lower Deck.

At 08.30 each morning we fell in on the parade ground to salute the flag, another occasion that could prove dangerously risible. This had nothing to do with the Union Jack itself. It was still over twenty years before it was to become a fun object and, although I would never have admitted it at the time, with the war on the turn there was something rather moving about its brisk and fluttering progress up the flagpole. The danger came immediately after the Marine band's version of the National Anthem. This, while rather elephantine, was efficient enough but it was followed, whether because of a general order or a local whim I never discovered, by the National Anthem of one of the Allies. When it was the turn of an occidental nation this sounded well enough, but the anthems of the East, involving as they did a different scale and rhythmic tradition, could lead to some uncertain and gong-punctuated noises.

Giggling is rarely a solitary occupation. It depends on mutual feedback; a painful attempt to suppress one's own snorts, tears and whinneys conflicting with an unpleasant desire to see one's co-giggler reinfected. I had in fact found a friend, someone to laugh with, and, for all my determination to crash the class-barriers, he was, typically enough, another public-school rating.

His real name was Graham but the class rechristened him Percy or The Professor. He had a high-pitched definitive voice, a very slightly androgynous walk and rather wide hips. We'd met in the

Camp dentist's waiting-room where I'd beem sitting prominently reading a collection of Osbert Sitwell's verse. Percy, from the other side of the room, told me that he thought less than nothing of Osbert and not much of Edith either. Auden was another matter. I hurriedly agreed with him – a selection of Auden was among my collection of lures and baits – and he trolled across the room to sit next to me, ignoring the friendly if derisive whistling and kissing noises of our fellow conscripts. These were not only because he was distinctly effeminate in both voice and gesture but also because he 'spoke posh'. This was a perpetual hazard in the Navy. The first day or two in a new mess one was constantly lampooned, especially at meals. 'I say, old man, be a sport and pass the jolly old salt what' – that kind of thing. It didn't last long, partly because it became boring if ignored but also because it was based on similar foundations to my own idealization of the working class en masse – unfamiliarity. For most of the Lower Deck a posh accent was equated with authority: the officers themselves, schoolmasters, bosses, BBC announcers, politicians and, in some cases, magistrates. Now for the first time the owner of a posh voice was vulnerable, equal. Yet because of this, provided we were neither openly arrogant nor patronizing, there grew up a collective pride in having us as part of a mess. This pride was sardonic rather than subservient. Long words, for example, were a never-failing reason for incredulous laughter or derision and, in our turn, many of us were tempted to play up, to ingratiate through exaggeration. Very often, running parallel to the mockery, a protective attitude developed. They felt sorry for us in our helplessness, the result of our sheltered upbringing. This too, at any rate for people like Percy and myself with our rather passive homosexual natures, appeared both flattering and pleasurable. The Chief himself projected both the mockery and the protective element.

'All right, Georgina,' he'd tell us while handing out jobs, 'you and Percy can go and clean out the 'eads together, but don't play with each other's squeegees.'

Where the Chief was completely inaccurate, however, was in suggesting that Percy and I had any interest in each other sexually. What we shared were the same tastes – a liking for butch and pretty heterosexual lads, or at any rate those who gave the appearance of heterosexuality.

This is not a case history, nor am I competent to analyse why, at the age of eighteen, I was still more or less completely gay, but perhaps a few pointers might help. To begin with my mother preferred in general the company of homosexuals. In provincial Liverpool they seemed to her to be more amusing, better company, more creative than most heterosexual Liverpudlians, and her fondness for the theatre and, more particularly, the theatrical atmosphere added to her circle a number of visiting firewomen all as camp as Chlöe. From my earliest years therefore I had learnt to equate wit and creativity with homosexuality even before I knew what it was. My father, it's true, was heterosexual but extremely tolerant. He once told me he'd been on a jury in a case of sodomy but that the accused had been acquitted. I asked him if they were guilty. 'Oh yes,' he said, 'but half the jury didn't think it was possible and the rest of us didn't think it mattered.' He had his own hearty heterosexual friends certainly, draft Bass drinkers in the main, but he saw them mostly in pubs. As host he presided over a largely gay ambiance or one where at any rate there was no stigma attached to deviance.

My loathed prep-school master, already remarked as initially responsible for my left-wing bias, confirmed me in my admiration for effeminacy through his hysterical and possibly ambivalent hatred of it. I was on one occasion slippered in front of the whole school for insisting, despite warnings, that I would prefer to go to the ballet than watch a game of rugger. In the face of such a brute I felt impelled, as far as a twelve-year-old boy could, to defend all those beautifully dressed, graceful, funny friends of my mother's.

At the same time that very prep-school, particularly after its evacuation to Shropshire at the beginning of the war, was athrob with sexual experimentation of all kinds. By the time I went to Stowe at the age of fourteen I was aware of (if in some instances uninitiated in) every variation of homosexual love-making. Yet at this date I hardly equated our pre-adolescent fumbling with those gay and witty young men I knew to be, in the fashionable slang of the time, pansies. Stowe bridged this gap, or at least an aesthetic set at Stowe did so. Wilde, Beardsley, Firbank, Proust became, by association, our mentors. We called our physical relationships 'affairs' and wrote each other poor if purple verses.

I left Stowe a convinced homosexual, believing and accepting that I would always remain one. I felt no shame, on the contrary I considered myself part of an elite, a freemasonry whose members held most of the keys to what was truly creative and exciting in the grown-up world. But, while genuinely attracted by boys, I was not inwardly entirely committed to my own sex. From quite a small boy I'd fantasized about girls, usually circus or pantomime performers and, at the cinema, the more obvious platinum blondes, bar-room whores and Busby Berkley chorines. Yet somehow I managed to convince myself that these fantasies in no way impinged on the purity of my homosexuality. The reason, I suspect now, for at the time I merely avoided correlating the two elements, was a pretty firm conviction that I would never be able to persuade a girl to say yes. My nature has always been to avoid any situation in which I thought I might fail.

I'd also developed several painful heterosexual crushes during my later childhood: a golden-skinned, violet-eyed Burne-Jones girl who'd spent a holiday with us in the Lake District the first summer of the war and, a year or two earlier, a sultry long-legged paying-guest, the daughter of a friend of my mother's who, whether provocatively or because she failed to recognize the explicit sexual feelings of a precocious ten-year-old, allowed me to sit and watch her put on her make-up wearing only her bra and cami-knicks, and for whom I bought Black Magic chocolates whenever I could afford it.

Yet these girls, and others less obsessively desired, were all eighteen or nineteen, in practical terms as inaccessible as the proud girl on the trapeze or the platinum-blonde Hollywood vamp. Boys on the other hand presented no such problem and, as I grew older, men too became viable. After all, it was they who might want me. I could refuse or accept and, even if I found them not especially attractive with their stubble, thinning hair and sagging flesh, I derived satisfaction from feeling myself wanted, from flattery, from having something to give. Ideally, however, I preferred those of my own age or a little younger, thought of myself as Oscar Wilde, making up what I might lack in beauty, for I was never physically vain, by charm and wit. I was also, for all my emotional passivity, in this area the active partner. A too-early and impetuously executed experience of sodomy had made it impossible for me to be buggered without fainting.

In the realm of friendship I was never committed solely to fellow pederasts. In fact my closest friends were usually, while of necessity uncensorious of my proclivities, heterosexual. In them, however, I sought an iconoclastic spirit. They all despised pomposity, taboos, fake emotions. They were expected to lead or goad me on to acts of outrage, to defy authority, to unmask humbug. I remained, during my naval days, in correspondence with several of them and we met, when on leave or stationed near each other, whenever possible. My mother, in general, tended to prefer my homosexual friends. They were better mannered, fell more readily under her spell and didn't, except in the sexual sense, attack or offend society so aggressively. She felt the others were apt to 'encourage me'.

Percy and I shared a common enthusiasm for the cinema and literature. He however was a classical music buff while I, despite a short-lived period in my teens when I sat, outwardly intense, inwardly bored silly, through a season of concerts at the Liverpool Philharmonic, was not. He was completely unmoved by jazz or blues, already my ruling passion, and like many extremely musical people was comparatively uninterested in the visual arts.

He was a severe literary critic, applying to individual poems, for example, a close analysis far removed from my own vague emotional response. I showed him with some pride a long poem on Prometheus I had written in Spenserian stanzas which I had entered successfully for a prize at school. 'It's no good,' he snapped, and showed me a poem by a schoolfriend of his about waiting at night on a lonely station platform. I had to admit it was a real poem not a limp romantic pastiche, but I didn't love him for it.

Films were a less contentious area. We were united in our admiration for Bogart in particular and the American crime thriller in general. We both admired Welles without reservation; at Stowe I had once reduced a small boy to tears because he had admitted to finding *Citizen Kane* boring after a Saturday night showing in the gym. We both loathed war-propaganda films; even the Bogart pictures of that period were often flawed by a five minute 'message' tacked on at the end; and we particularly abhorred the cycle of Hollywood 'occupation' movies with their unpleasant mixture of schmaltz, sadism and complete unreality.

We both enjoyed, although perhaps with a certain con-descension, low pubs and music halls. Although we quite liked the ENSA shows in the camp theatre, we preferred a small, extremely tatty hall in the town itself where the comics were both blue and hopeless, the jugglers dropped their props, the performing dogs ran off stage, and the chorines, some openly chewing gum supplied no doubt by American airmen from one of the nearby USAF bases, were just as openly contemptuous of their simple routines.

If asked at that time my aspirations I would have said, despite Percy's rejections of 'Prometheus', 'to be a writer'. After a few pints, and I became inebriated in those days on an enviably small quantity of cheap flat mild, I was convinced that I understood the poetic significance of everything: the mahogany and engraved glass, the pool of beer on the bar, the faded fly-blown pre-war advert for gin, cigarette smoke, overheard fragments of con-versation. Sitting in that music hall, enchanted by a tatty backcloth of a 'modernistic' cityscape or noting how the foot-lights by reversing the pattern of light and shade on a comedian's face emphasized the dead, puppet-like quality of his act, I would say to myself very solemnly that 'one day I must get this all down'.

I didn't actually write anything however. Admiration for others inhibited me. I believed that until I felt myself able to equal the interplay between inner and outer reality in the opening paragraphs of Joyce's *Ulysses* there was no point in starting, and I wasn't quite ready for that yet. One day, I was convinced, I would sit down with a notebook and several sharp pencils and write, without hesitancy, the opening sentences of the greatest novel of the century. Until then I was 'living', 'absorbing impressions', and limbering up for the obligatory spell of silence, exile and cunning at some later date. The point was that, like most protected youths with literary interests, both Percy and I saw everything through established writers' eyes. In Skegness, admittedly more lively than most resorts due to the presence of nearby military and naval establishments, and no longer heavily fortified against invasion, we would chant 'August for the people' as we reeled its near-empty streets.

At a 'talent night' in camp Percy, despite his indifference to jazz, condescended to accompany me on 'Frankie and Johnnie', a ballad he would allow some virtues as Auden had included it in his anthology of folk poetry. Percy's classical training meant that his version was rather stiff and academic. My singing was more enthusiastic than tuneful, but we won for all that and were asked to stage a repeat performance in the Petty Officers' mess by our Chief, where we were made much of and treated to a great deal of beer. Yet despite our success I was unable to convince Percy that there was anything in jazz. I was not however alone in my enthusiasm. I soon found out that the rediscovery of Morton, Oliver, early Louis and Bessie Smith was not, as I imagined, a local phenomenon confined to a small group at Stowe. When I whistled, recognizably if only approximately, a chorus from Louis' 'Kneedrops' in the NAAFI, it was identified by a young Glaswegian and later, after I'd sung 'Frankie and Johnnie', other ratings came up and admitted to a keen interest in the music. Early jazz, it seemed, was a widespread minority passion which cut across all traditional class and cultural barriers and through it, without thinking about it, I discovered the key to that door I had been trying to force: communication with some of those whom my mother, reacting to my insistent and provocative hymning of their praises in every letter I sent home, had taken to describing as 'your friends, the working classes'.

At the end of our second week, the time we were due to be transferred to Ipswich, we were told that there was a bottleneck and that we would be staying at Skegness for up to five weeks more to do intensive square-bashing, PT and some elementary seamanship. I went home for a few days' leave. Shortly after I got back to camp we had a nasty shock. The reason for our hold-up became clear. The Navy had drawn too many Ordinary Seamen. We were to be made either cooks, writers or stewards or, if unsuitable for any of these roles, redirected into the Army.

The explanation was, in human terms, something to be grateful for. The number of casualties among naval personnel during the D-Day invasion hadn't been anything like as heavy as expected, in fact almost negligible. In consequence the Navy had quite enough fully-trained ratings and didn't need us. At the time though, while perfectly aware that this was why we were to be transferred, I can remember feeling nothing but frustration. Cooks, stewards and writers didn't wear bellbottoms. They wore a uniform rather like a shabby chauffeur, dark blue with a white shirt, black tie and a peaked cap. Furthermore the writers, the branch into which despite no ability whatsoever in maths or methodical clerical work I was enrolled, contained a majority of the one class I believed it somehow perfectly defensible to despise, the *petit bourgeoisie*.

In my indifference to the progress of the war, first at school and then in the Navy, I was by no means alone among my generation. Beyond the normal self-absorption of adolescents, I think our failure to consider the implications of losing was based on an inability to conceive this as a possibility. This was not surprising, even for those of us who thought of ourselves as rebels. Since our childhood we had been indoctrinated, both openly and implicitly, to believe in Britain's superiority.

Being half-Jewish, I'd every reason to fear and hate Hitler and was, theoretically at any rate, an anti-Fascist, but the tone of

British propaganda during the Second World War, at any rate until the discovery of the extermination camps, was either practical – 'Dig for Victory', 'Lend to Defend the Right to be Free', 'Britain Can Take It' – or mocking. Hitler, Goering and the rest were ridiculed in cartoons, songs and comedy shows on the wireless. 'Adolph, you've bitten off much more than you can chew,' sang Arthur Askey. Fougasse's warnings against careless talk showed the Nazi leaders sitting rather cosily on a bus listening to a pair of garrulous housewives giving away secrets on the seat in front. There was none of the anti-German hysteria of the 1914–18 war. No dachshunds were kicked in the street. Beethoven, far from being banned, was responsible for the V for Victory musical symbol. Rommel was even promoted as 'a good German', a worthy opponent, and the German troops respected where the Italians, with their admirable lack of enthusiasm for the conflict, were despised.

I was too young to take in Dunkirk, but found Churchill's rhetoric and *persona* curiously unreal. Even the bombing, and I sat through several weeks of that in my grandmother's cellar under the block of flats next to our house in Liverpool (the smell of damp still evokes the crump of falling bombs), felt more like a natural phenomenon than the destructive and deliberate work of man. 'Jerry's late tonight,' people would say almost affectionately. Nor did the hearty joviality or purposeful grim tones of the newsreel commentators make the war less distant or more real. I was still a child when it started and it seemed to have been going on for ever. The disappearance of bananas meant as much to us as the Battle of Britain.

On the other hand my contempt for the lower-middle classes had nothing to do with the war, nor was it confined to me. It's an old heresy, and one that still exists, to believe that the upper classes and the working classes are alike in their freedom from convention, are somehow 'real', whereas the lower-middle classes are the prisoners of their own aspirations, castrated by their pretensions, fair game for teasing and shocking. Through holding this belief it is possible to suck up to the aristocracy and patronize the working classes and feel unsnobbish when in fact indulging one's snobbery shamelessly at the expense of suburban commuters and their families.

Worse, most of this snobbery is based on taste, on the crooking of little fingers and non-U vocabulary. It's not really the sense of propriety, the admittedly narrow outlook, the opportunist morality that goads the intellectual, and all these defects are perhaps more strongly in evidence in the suburbs than in any other sector of the community. It's the garden gnomes, the love of light classical music, the chiming doorbells, the ritualistic washing of the car, these are the butts, the excuse for mockery. Of course the assertive belief that their standards are right, that their measure of taste is unassailable, can be irritating. In the Navy I was constantly under attack from the *petit bourgeoisie* for preferring jazz to, say, the 'Warsaw Concerto' and I retaliated cruelly and contemptuously, wrote home sneering at those I called 'the tomato-growers', while at the same time deceiving myself I was socially without prejudice. To find myself a writer, a clerk, in a badly-cut suit with a collar and tie depressed me immeasurably and, to be truthful, I was aware too that dressed like that would make me an object of less interest to homosexuals. For them, traditionally, bellbottoms were in themselves something of an aphrodisiac. There was nothing to be done, however, and having handed in our ordinary seamen's uniforms and drawn our hated fore-and-aft rig, Percy and I were sent to do the first part of our writers' training course at a camp on the outskirts of Malvern.

Chapter 2

HMS *Duke*, a shore establishment, had been built as such and lacked in consequence those bizarre touches which helped relieve the austerity of the requisitioned Butlin Camps. It stood a little outside the town and depressed me instantly. For the first few weeks Percy and I were in different classes and couldn't even go on shore leave together. Later we were able to appear at 'Commander's Requests and Defaulters' for permission to rejoin each other and, at the price of a raised eyebrow from the officer on duty and a confirmatory smile from our Petty Officer, our request was granted.

On board, as we soon learnt to refer to the rigid geometry of the camp, we were taught nothing as yet in connection with our future role as the Navy's clerks but, in the company of cooks and stewards, sweated and cursed yet again through our basic training. This was reasonable enough. HMS *Duke* was after all the intake establishment for all fore-and-aft men and, by relinquishing our bellbottoms, we were officially new entries. It was dispiriting though and lacked that salty obscenity which had made the rigours of Skegness acceptable.

A season in hell among the tomato-growers was how I saw it, and my sense of snobbish outrage was fed by discovering that whereas seamen turned in wearing their underwear, a practice which struck me as cheerfully squalid and which I soon adopted in preference to my pyjamas, my fellow clerks wore pyjamas *over* their underwear.

The traditional cry 'Show a leg' derives from the sexually permissive eighteenth century when sailors were allowed to cohabit with women between decks. On this command, the hairless leg of a doxy extending sleepily over the edge of a hammock entitled its owner to snooze on. They shouted 'Show a leg' at 6.30 every morning on HMS *Duke*, but mechanically and with no indication of awareness as to its original meaning. In fact the whole rhetoric of this bout of training lacked edge or colour. Our very Petty Officer, dispirited by the slightly priggish reaction of the more straightlaced writer trainees, abandoned any pretence to originality and fell back on those well-worn military cliches already familiar to me from a number of wartime films in the Crown Film Unit tradition.

'If yer don't pull your fuckin' socks up,' he'd shout with the minimum of conviction, 'I'll 'ave yew runnin' up and down that fuckin' 'ill! It needs flattenin' !!'

The hill in question was truly enormous. It towered over the town nestling on its lower slopes, and this should at least have given the Petty Officer's uninventive threat the virtue of maximum exaggeration. It didn't, because the Malvern Hills, while certainly steep and at that time of the year generously splashed with extravagant browns and oranges, managed to avoid the grandeur to which their scale entitled them. They had the look of those reproductions of watercolours you could buy from the larger branches of Boots; an easily digested aesthetic calculated to appeal to those retired military men and elderly ladies with small private incomes who had elected to spend their later years in Malvern's innumerable private hotels and boarding houses and were largely responsible for the spa's air of moribund gentility.

The presence of a naval camp, while no doubt accepted as a patriotic necessity, may have initially distressed the residents, but the Navy's choice of personnel was as tactful as possible. The largely abstemious writers, in their very appearance reassuringly suggestive of more prosperous times when a chauffeur waited to receive his orders for the day, sipped their halfs of bitter quietly in the orderly public bars. They posed no threat. If HMS *Duke* had been a training camp for Glaswegian stokers the recognized need for sacrifice in our hour of need would have been stretched to breaking point.

The only evidence in Malvern that the average age of the entire civilian population wasn't around seventy, was provided by a number of schools in the area. In particular there was a girls' school, which allowed its sixth form out on Saturday afternoons. They'd walk, whispering excitedly arm in arm, up and down the mountainous High Street, sit in cafés lost in moony reveries or, after mysterious glances and long pauses, burst into irrepressible shared giggles. Percy and I would walk past them as we strolled the streets waiting impatiently for the pubs or cinema to open. We'd sit, sipping coffee and watching them tucking into powdered scrambled eggs on toast or 'fancy cakes' made from soya bean flour and filled with synthetic cream. Percy found them irritating, but I, with my more ambivalent sexual identity, was mildly excited by their purple blazers, shirts and ties, grey flannel skirts and black woollen stockings and would sometimes murmur with wistful lasciviousness a phrase I'd heard used by great aunts when I was a small boy – 'She married straight out of the school room.'

We endured out training and, although my sluttish appearance led at times to a mild reproach, we could by now perform our drill and tie our repertoire of knots without even thinking about it. I had expected to be morally shocked by bayonet practice, the only addition to the Skegness curriculum, and no doubt had I been conscripted into a fighting regiment I would have been appalled. Here, however, among my fellow pen-pushers, the pale cooks and weedy stewards, the exercise lacked all realism. Even the Petty Officer in charge found it difficult to keep up the pretence of ferocity. 'H'imagine you've got a German h'on the h'end of that,' he'd yell as we jabbed feebly away at the suspended straw-filled sacks, but it was perfectly obvious that neither he nor we could imagine any such thing. Neither, given our naval futures in pay depot, galley or officers' mess, was the situation likely to arise.

Life in camp was a kind of limbo, not unbearable exactly but more or less unpleasant depending on how early or cold it was, or whether what we were doing involved painful physical effort. Yet I can remember one moment when I was suddenly aware of being intensely, almost impossibly happy. I was one of a number of ratings marched down to a railway siding to transfer some stores, potatoes I believe, from a goods van to one of the camp lorries. It was a warm and sunny October afternoon. I was eighteen, and somehow the stationary, rusty goods train, the overgrown banks of the railway cutting, the noise of the cinders crunching under our feet, the blue cloudless sky, the rhythm of the work, a sense of physical well-being – all fused to become one of those rare, almost painfully ecstatic experiences which stay in the mind forever, and are all the more mysterious for having no logical or overtly emotional explanation.

'Liberty Men' is the name for sailors on shore leave and once at liberty Percy and I headed for the cinema. This formed part of what would now be called a complex: a handsome Victorian building with a heavily-marbled hall under a fine iron and glass roof and with a fountain of nymphs and cherubs extinguished for the duration, for at a time when patriots were advised to paint a line only a few inches above the bottom of their baths no fountains played or trickled. The cinema was small but, whether by chance or because whoever booked the films was an enthusiast, the programmes were uniformly excellent. Bette Davis in *Look Stranger* sent us beside ourselves with camp enthusiasm, and it was here too that I first watched that great mutilated masterpiece,

The Magnificent Ambersons. We sat in the warm dark almost alone, for even at that time when the cinemas were always full, Welles was box office poison. So it was for us that the Ambersons lost their fortune and to us that the master, having introduced his actors and technical credits, thundered out that last great megalomanic cry – 'I wrote and directed this picture. My name is Orson Welles.'

One afternoon on shore leave, alone for once (perhaps Percy was on leave in Aldershot), I went to look at a British Council travelling exhibition of Blake and Fuseli. Both were artists I admired; both after all had been praised by the Surrealists, or by Herbert Read at any rate, and the latter provided a chapter in Sacheverel Sitwell's *Splendours and Miseries*, a book I'd chosen as my prize for writing the poem about Prometheus which Percy had so despised.

Among others peering at the pictures was a family, the father ruddy and bearded, dressed in the tweedy homespun style of an Osbert Lancaster Hampstead intellectual, his short pleasant-looking red-haired wife and a small son. 'That,' I heard the man announce firmly and resonantly, 'is a bloody fine piece of work by Billy Blake,' and he jabbed with the end of his pipe towards one of Fuseli's nightmare ladies smiling in a most ambivalently malicious way under her elaborate coiffure.

Absurdly, and on occasion dangerously, I've never been able to stop myself pedantically correcting people's incorrect information. Once, aged about ten, I'd narrowly avoided having my ears boxed by an irate father at the Liverpool Zoo when I'd told him that 'dat leopard' he was pointing out to his small son was in fact a jaguar. This time too I sailed in. 'Actually Fuseli,' I murmured. The man took it well. He looked for a moment at the single sheet of the catalogue to check up, found out I was right and shouted, 'Bugger me! So it is, and who are you?' I told him my name and was asked to tea. His name, he told me, was Donald Cowie and he was an author. He was a publisher too. Fed up with what he called 'the bloody freemasonry of publishers' he'd founded the Tantivy Press and, with remarkable persistence and serendipity, had unearthed pre-war stores of very beautiful paper lying in small and mostly rural paper mills. On this he had printed and published a large body of his own work, most of it light satirical verse in a traditional mode and, as bookshops were starved for anything to put on sale in those paper-rationed days, he did extremely well.

Theoretically, as an enthusiastic if ill-informed admirer of the Surrealists and a rather precious young man in general, I should have detested both his work and him. I was, however, in part impressed by his scatological and sexual Rabelaisian turn of phrase, and equally won over by his kindness and the way in which he treated my aspirations to become a writer with apparent gravity. Always a chameleon, I found myself, in his company, assuming a bluff and noisy neo-Georgianism redolent of beer and wenches and long tramps through damp bracken. I was impressed too at his output (albeit self-published), and by his friendship with the then celebrated Professor Joad, a popularizing philosopher, the mainstay of the BBC's Brains Trust, and, according to Donald, as randy a as goat, as drunk as a judge, and much given to climbing up lamposts and similar japes.

Later, Joad was savagely discredited, quite absurdly in my view, for riding on a train without paying for a ticket, but at that time he was a national figure almost as famous as Tommy Handley, and much imitated for his philosophical catch phrase, 'It all depends what you mean by . . .' and his rapid, precise, if rather high-pitched delivery. For the friendship of a writer who knew Joad, I was prepared to put aside any reservations. Not so Percy. I only took him there once, but it was a sour disaster. Percy's literary seriousness was appalled by Donald's facility, while his equally puritanical homosexuality was offended by Donald's uxorious celebration of heterosexual monogamy. There was one sentence in particular, a sentence which began 'Last night my fingers were exploring the nocturnal interstices of my wife . . .' which turned him crimson with embarrassed distaste. His comments afterwards were withering on both an aesthetic and personal level. We had begun to drift apart.

Not that Donald Cowie was the sole reason for that. More important was a new friendship with a tall boy from Wolverhampton, a warm-hearted, slightly cynical person with a lop-sided grin and the look of a younger Joseph Cotten. His name was Harry Wakefield and like me, but with more natural aptitude, he was training to be a writer. I fell head-over-heels for Harry and he, while interested only in girls, was prepared to accept my adoration in return for the amusement I provided him and, I believe, genuine affection.

All through my life I have been attracted by people like Harry Wakefield, at first, although fruitlessly, in the sexual field but soon (sex more or less sublimated if not all that far below the surface) as platonic friends.

Harry knew a great deal more about jazz than I. It was he who pointed out that if I really liked improvisation above all else, both Muggsy Spanier and, come to that, Duke Ellington and Jelly Roll Morton relied in the main on arrangements, so in praising them I was talking nonsense and must either revise my opinions or discard them. This really threw me, but he added that as, within the scored passages, there were plenty of holes for improvising, why not admire both their skill as composers *and* the brilliance of their soloists? This view seemed and seems to me extremely sensible and although for many years I remained suspicious of the saxophone, I soon became less rigid and more open.

At all events it was with Harry's star in the ascendancy, and Percy's in decline, that we finished our basic training as writers and were sent home on leave. As for the Cowies, we kept up a correspondence for some time and indeed, when a sortie North on a bookselling expedition took them near Liverpool, I was able to repay some of their hospitality by asking my parents to put them up. My mother didn't 'care for his beard'. My father was very amused and indeed impressed by the fact that, under various pseudonyms, Donald wrote all the critical puffs on the dust-covers of his own work and, more conventionally, the publishers' blurb as well. But distance and diverging views soon put an end to our letters, and I never met or indeed heard of him again.

Chapter 3

My leaves in Liverpool have by now fused into one long leave.
The Blitz was long over and the northern port had never suffered
under the doodle-bug attacks which had, until the success of
D-Day, made life in London and the South so nerve-wracking a
phenomenon. Still the sense of being at war persisted: the
gaping bomb-sites as yet nude of weeds, the partial black-out,
the notices in the butchers' windows announcing what numbers
in which streets were entitled to offal. On arriving at Lime
Street Station I'd board a one or thirty-three tram-car, and walk
with my kitbag over my shoulder and my ditty-box (a small
cardboard suitcase) in my hand towards the comforts of home.
For ten days or so I'd see my relations, chat to my small sister,
stroll the public parks of my childhood, and go to the theatre
with my mother or a friend of hers, a fat, highly literate and

intelligent queen who had decided to take in hand my education and plied me with books, magazines and advice.

At the end of each leave, my woollen underwear restored to approximate whiteness (for my own efforts at 'dobying' never achieved more than what I called 'hammock grey'), I'd stagger back down to Lime Street to face the long journey back to wherever I was stationed. 'Leave,' they told us frequently in the Navy, 'is a privilege, not a right.'

This time my destination was the writers' training camp at Wetherby, a small town near Leeds in frozen Yorkshire. It was the week after Christmas.

It wasn't exactly that I'd no intention of passing my exams at HMS *Demetrius*, an establishment appropriately far from the sea. My moments of revolt, rare but extreme, have always been public, either the end result of accumulated angry frustration or the unpremeditated effect of a rush of adrenalin through the system. The notion of deliberately faking stupidity was foreign to me. Nor, in this case, was it necessary. My mathematical sense has always been shaky. I can't add up a row of figures twice and reach the same answer. I'm not however one of those who try to present this failing as a virtue: the proof of unworldly seer-like preoccupations. It's very irritating and has cost me dear. I comforted myself on this occasion that at least I'd pointed it out in advance to those who had insisted on allocating me to such an unsuitable role and did my best, given a persistent inability to concentrate on something which doesn't interest me, to work out how much pay less tax would be earned by a 1st Lieutenant, acting-captain of a motor-torpedo boat, with a wife, two children and a dependent mother. The Lieutenant, had he existed, would have become somewhat nervous as each pay-day drew near, never knowing whether to expect a salary rather higher than an Admiral of the Fleet, or considerably less than the expectations of a Victorian crossing sweeper during a heatwave.

As each exam approached I reacted, as I'd often done at school, by a series of genuine but undoubtedly psychosomatic diseases. Glands swelled, teeth abscessed, flu struck. Harry and Percy were almost ready to pass out before I'd taken and failed my first test.

Happily, the camp's Training Commander, a squat, ruddy-faced, blue-jowelled Jewish officer given to twinkling, found me absurdly amusing or, more accurately, amusingly absurd. I'd first come to his attention when a prudish lady-sorter in the Wetherby post office had sent back with a complaint an envelope addressed to my mother which I'd decorated with some sub-Rex Whistlerian cherubs, modestly, indeed almost vestigially hung. He'd returned this to me, forced, because the complaint had been official, to issue at least a formal reprimand, but making it perfectly clear that he thought the woman was a prurient fool. He suggested that in future I confined my *putti* to inside the envelope. From then on he kept a sardonic eye on my anti-progress. He gave the impression of boredom and impatience with his job, and at least my passionate defence of my right to give male cherubs appropriate if minute sexual organs made a change from deciding what to do about ratings late off-shore, or cooks apprehended smuggling out a pound of butter on weekend leave.

Our next encounter seemed more serious. At Christmas, after a beery dinner served to us, as was the naval custom during that period of traditional misrule, by the officers, I and Harry Wakefield fell asleep on the same bunk and were roughly awoken by a fiercely heterosexual Warrant Officer who had long suspected and resented my propensities. He put us on a charge but the Commander would have none of it.

'Far too drunk to have done anything about it even if they'd wanted to,' he commented dismissively. Our accuser reddened, and Harry and I, he with justifiable innocence, me at any rate technically not guilty, saluted, turned about and marched out of the room.

In between working up to being ill during exams or recovering after them, I quite enjoyed Wetherby. Physical exercise was minimal. Football was voluntary, and even the obligatory twenty minutes of PT before breakfast required no more effort than was necessary in order not to freeze. The classes were boring enough but there was a reasonably warm canteen, a piano player stumbling through boogie-woogie, the tick-tock of ping-pong balls, Harry or Percy to chatter to over the watery pints of NAAFI mild. The war too had begun to swing in our favour. We didn't talk about it much, but it meant a diminution of possible risk and that was cheering.

So we sat, played dominoes, talked about jazz or painting, speculated as to why the smoke was blue when it curled up from the end of a cigarette but grey when expelled from the lungs, indulged in horse-play, listened to Bechet or Jelly Roll on a gramophone borrowed from the chaplain; inadequately, in my case, washed our underpants, gave blood to a travelling unit known as 'the mobile Dracula wagon', slept heavily on 'make and mends', masturbated often, and got drunk in Leeds or Harrogate.

Harry and I didn't often go into Harrogate. A safe refuge for the elderly, it seemed too like another Malvern, although we were temporarily impressed and amused by its enormous Edwardian hotels where a few old ladies ate their meagre lunches in the Baroque wastes of the underheated diningrooms, and a palm court trio, wearing cardigans against the cold, scraped out selections from 'Floradora' or the 'Yeoman of the Guard'.

We much preferred Leeds, a wide-open city with enough tarts and drunkenness to earn itself one of those 'revealing' articles in the *News of the World*. Although the war continued, there was now no question of an air-raid and modified street lighting had been re-introduced. This made our reeling sorties from pub to dance-hall to pub to café to YMCA or Salvation Army hostel less hazardous, and revealed also the Victorian Gothic fantasy of the town. In the city square, a platoon of solid nymphs held lamps aloft. There were elegant glass-roofed arcades to explore and a huge town-hall, a sooty metaphor for the civic pride of the High Victorian dead.

I discovered eventually that you could take a tram out to a large Elizabethan manor house on the outskirts of the city where the Corporation housed many of its treasures including what was, for those days, a rather adventurous modern collection.

The tram-ride itself was a dreamlike pleasure. The last few stops were among woods, the rattling tram was old and Emmet-like, with an ornate spiral staircase and little panels of engraved blue and red glass above the windows. The house, Temple Newsham, had Latin mottoes picked out in stone around the parapets of the great courtyard. It was usually empty, and Harry and I wandered its Crimson rooms full of Rubens and Canalettos and roped-off eighteenth-century furniture, and spent a long time admiring the Graham Sutherlands, Henry Moores and Paul Nashes in the modern collection. Later, after I had met the Surrealist Group in London, I rapidly recanted my admiration for these artists, apostates all, and shamefacedly tucked away those oblong Penguin Modern Masters which extolled their work, but at Wetherby I still found anything 'modern' admirable.

Culture in the afternoon then, a habit I was to keep intermittently throughout my naval career because, for one thing, it was very economical, and vice, or at any rate aspirations to vice, in the evenings.

Vice in Leeds, that last winter of the European war, centred for us on The Dick Turpin, a garish public house in Thirties' cream and green, not far from the city centre. Percy came once and didn't like it, but Harry and I did, and in no time were on friendly terms with the rather drab and pathetic little whores and their lord and master, a Spanish pimp called Tony Angelo.

As to why I was so impressed, the answer, I suppose, lay in my association of whores with the Storyville era in the history of New Orleans jazz. To talk to real whores and pimps seemed to me to create some kind of spiritual link with Buddy Bolden, Tom Anderson, Lulu White and Jelly Roll Morton.

There was one girl with whom I became quite friendly. She charged, she told me, three guineas, a curiously pedantic sum, but threw in breakfast and kept the place spotless (or so she said, for at three guineas a throw I hadn't the means to find out even if I'd had the inclination). She was worried because she had no Identity Card. She despised goodtime girls 'who "go" for nothing'. I listened to her for hours, hearing the tinkle of the whorehouse piano in my mind's ear, and, about once a night, in exchange for buying him a gin and orange, I was allowed a few moments' audience with Tony Angelo himself. Dressed in a wide-lapelled black-market suit, wearing a mauve silk shirt, kipper tie and pointed leather shoes, sporting an amazing amount of jewellery, heavily-scented, his Brylcreamed hair worn long for those days, his hairline moustache almost invisible in its precision, he seemed to me the most glamorous person I'd ever met. His arrogance too was God-like. When I asked him, rather nervously, about his reaction to that article in the *News of the World*, he'd shrugged dismissively. 'I not frightened of those beeg fat City Halderman,' he said examining a beautifully manicured nail, 'I know too much haybout them.' City corruption too, I thought to myself. Here I am talking to a man described in the newspaper as 'a slimy foreign beast earning a fat living from battoning on to women of a certain sort', and he feels perfectly safe because he knows too much about the City Fathers. Orgies in the Mayor's parlour perhaps? Gross old men in their sock suspenders chasing Tony Angelo's tarts round a solid mahogany table with the mace on it? I wished he'd tell me more, but, the gin and orange once dispatched, the audience was at an end.

One night too, five vicars marched in. Hearty and unshockable, they had come to fight the good fight.

'Come to save me fookin' soul!' yelled a very drunken girl from Bradford.

'If I can, sister,' said the leader of the troop bravely.

A year later, my atheism confirmed by Surrealist doctrine, and my anti-clericalism fed at the same source, I would perhaps have felt it necessary to insult the Men of God in imitation of Benjamin Peret in that famous photograph, but that night I was prepared to dismiss their prayers and hymns among the indifferent clientèle of The Dick Turpin as 'noble but misled'. I wrote as much to my mother, adding pompously that I found 'negative stupidity and the belief that civilization was a refrigerator in every home, worse sins than drunkenness and copulation'.

I was in love with squalor then, and scoured the city for it, usually finishing the night drinking Camp coffee in a filthy little café. We'd struck up an acquaintance with an old woman there called 'Cigarette Liz'. She wore a cap and stank of mildewed pennies, a complaint she put down to a canker.

'Me 'usbands used ter beat me,' she croaked. 'All me 'usbands did, but they all knew about me money and drew out insurance policies. There'll be four or five of 'em wrangling over me when I'm gone.'

I listened attentively. She went on: 'There was a rat wot lived in me tent when I camped out on the waste-land.' The Waste Land! The rat's foot stirring the bones in the cellar in 'The Straw Men'! The literary echoes produced an immediate know-all *frisson*. I must remember to point them out to Percy next day, I told myself.

'Did you feed 'im, Liz?' asked the enormous, pregnant proprietress; her ninth she'd told me.

'Yes. On fish. You should have seen 'im swim. Fookin' water-rat he wus.'

Dickensian cackling.

'There was a rat wot used to come in 'ere,' said the café owner, not to be outdone. 'Used to come in this very shop and go "wee wee" at me. "'Ere's me rat," I'd say, but the young chap wot 'elped with the chips said, "Bugger you and your rat!" That's what 'e said, "Bugger you and your rat!" '

Harry, like most of the heterosexuals I became fond of during that period of my life, did his best to convince me that girls were better value. In fact, while at Wetherby, I was not particularly active anyway. Most of the writers were extremely prudish, and although Percy and I had once spent an evening out with two stokers from the camp's ship's company, it had led to little more than some heavy petting behind the boiler house, for by the time we came back on board we were far too drunk to get anywhere at all. Yet Henry's proselytism continued. It wasn't that he was in any way censorious. It was just that he believed it to be lack of heterosexual experience rather than choice or inclination which dictated my propensities.

With what he believed my interests at heart, he would

occasionally drag me away from The Dick Turpin and we'd spend the evening cruising a flyblown dance-hall where, under a revolving globe of facetted mirror-glass, we'd try to chat up those girls too homely not to have been commandeered by the infinitely more glamorous and far better paid American service men. One night, just before Christmas, we scored; Harry's girl being, of the two, by far the prettier. This I accepted as inevitable, Harry being not only better-looking but more at ease when it came to exchanging that mocking *badinage* which conversation demanded. We left the dance-hall after 'The King' and bought them fish and chips. Then, following a rather inconclusive 'snog' under some railway arches, put them on the last train to a nearby woollen mill town where they lived and worked.

Before their train left, Harry's girl had proposed a date, mine looking considerably less eager, and we'd agreed to make a foursome of it some ten days later. On our train back to Wetherby I'd expressed considerable dismay at the prospect. I'd found my experiences the reverse of satisfactory, let alone aphrodisiac. It's true we'd kissed but, as I told Harry, her mouth tasted of batter from the fish and chips we'd bought combined most unpleasantly with the Fulnana cachous she'd been sucking. Furthermore I didn't like having her virulent red lipstick smeared all over my face and collar. There was no question either of 'going further' – a tentative attempt to feel her breast had been repulsed with a sharp slap across the wrist. Not that this had worried me particularly. She'd seemed to me both lumpy and pasty, her conversation limited to Palais catchphrases, and she'd cost me a lot of money as well. I added that personally I'd have soon spent it getting pissed in The Dick Turpin.

I sat back on the dusty cushions of the unheated local train and sulked. In the mirror above Harry's head I could see the lipstick smeared across my collar. Harry laughed. Had I forgotten we were going on leave, next week? They'd no intention of keeping the date, no more than we had. That was just a polite convention. His didn't come across either. A prick-teaser and a waste of time. The next evening ashore we'd go to The Dick Turpin.

Christmas came. Paperchains in the NAAFI. Carols in the tin church. Harry was particularly affectionate as he knew I'd felt silly and inadequate, and he thought it was perhaps his fault. It may have been this that persuaded him to let me share his bunk after our turkey and plum pudding; an act of kindly expiation which led us close to the edge of disaster. Then, when that half of the trainees who'd been on leave returned, the rest of us set off for our four days at home; Harry to Wolverhampton, and me to Liverpool.

I was due back on 31 December and, no doubt because another exam was looming up, developed en route an agonizing toothache. It was a Sunday, and after I'd changed stations, running between City and Central, each step jogging my tooth most painfully and sweat pouring down my face, I discovered that my efforts had been in vain. I had three minutes to spare to catch the nine o'clock train to Wetherby. It being a holiday, the ticket collector told me with that smug satisfaction which all petty officials derive from transmitting unwelcome information, it wasn't running. The next one was 6 a.m. 'A lot of your lads made the same mistake,' he added. 'They weren't best pleased. None of 'em!'

I turned, resigned to a night at the YMCA, to find myself facing two viragos.

'Why didn't yer turn up to keep yer date today?' snapped mine.

'Aye, and where's 'Arry?' demanded the other.

Harry's 'polite convention' had crumbled. Clearly his charm had persuaded his girl that he had meant it and she'd dragged mine along to prove it. Typically enough it was mine who was the more furious. I calmed them down – unexpected leave (lie); here was my pass to prove it; no way to get in touch (true); Harry desperate but his mother was none too well (two more lies). Gradual resignation on the part of the girls.

Would they like a cup of tea? Yes. Their train wasn't until 10.20 p.m., and so off we went, and, with no need to prove myself sexually, we had quite a pleasant three-quarters of an hour, chatting away in a café near the station. They told me about their work, 'the toil' they called it, in a woollen mill, and what film stars they liked and how one of them, Harry's, had been going steady with a soldier but had broken it off because he was 'so thick', and then, at 10.15, we strolled back companionably to the station, arm in arm, and I felt quite a dog. Two girls, one on each arm. Even my tooth hardly bothered me.

They got the tickets out of their Dorothy bags and we approached the barrier. Another official, dead ringer of mine, smiled with grim delight. 'Aye, 10.20 *most* Sundays,' he agreed, 'but Good Fridays, Christmas Day and New Year's Eve she pulls out at 10.10. There won't be another now until morning.'

Both girls burst into instant hysterics.

'What will me dad say!'

'Oh bloody 'eck!'

'You've never seen me dad wild!'

I tried to reassure them. Led them to a telephone box and sent off identical telegrams to their fathers: 'Don't worry. Missed train. Spending the night in Girls Friendly Society Hostel.' 'Love Barbara' in one case; 'Love Margaret' in the other.

The woman taking it down, recognizing a masculine voice, read them back to me with disapproving scepticism. She also told me neither telegram would get there before morning anyway, but I thought it judicious to keep this from Barbara and Margaret, who were beginning to look, if not cheerful, at any rate glumly resigned.

I looked up the hostel and found it to be in a distant suburb. Taxis were predictably hard to find but at last we got one going more or less in the right direction, although we had to share it with two randy soldiers and an old drunk, who kept asking what was wrong with a drink on New Year's Eve at defensively frequent intervals. We eventually found the hostel, all lights off and in no way suggesting anything even minimally friendly. I rang and knocked for ten minutes. Eventually a sour elderly woman answered the door. She was in a dressing gown and a filthy temper. At first she refused to take them in. 'Very well,'

I said, 'my mother is a prominent social worker in Liverpool. She'd be *most* interested to hear that two girls had been refused admittance on a dark winter's night. Could I have your name, madam?'

Yet again that unfair confidence which is the birth-right of the middle classes won out. She took them in, both expressing their gratitude, she admonishing them for their noisiness, rattling out the rules of the establishment.

So there I was alone in the laurel-haunted drive of a large Victorian private house on the edge of a city. My bad tooth, forgotten during the necessity for action, reminded me of its existence.

It took me forty minutes to walk back into Leeds. The streets were full of maniacs, people being sick, others roaring out the songs of the day. I caught myself reflected, looking desperate, in the window of a big store with a street lamp behind me. I'd never felt more miserable in my life.

The YMCA was full but they let me sit on a wooden chair with my tooth giving me hell. I caught the 6 a.m. train back to camp, but had no trouble for being late as so many others were in the same boat. The tooth came out next day. It had abscessed badly, and they used procaine, a new local drug. I was well enough to take the exam, but predictably failed it. Harry and Percy had meanwhile both passed their finals.

A month later, the Commander sent for me. I'd flunked it again. Harry and Percy had both been drafted. There seemed no way I would ever escape from HMS *Demetrius*. I was beginning to feel a certain despair.

'Quite clearly,' he said, looking through my file. 'There's no point in you going on like this. I suggest you get back into bellbottoms; in fact I've applied for you to do so. I don't think they'll say no and I can see you're not exactly against the idea' – this was obvious as I was grinning broadly and trying hard not to jump up and down – 'Meanwhile you can join the ship's company on a temporary basis and make yourself useful in the galley.' I saluted and once outside his office began to leap and gambol along the neat paths like a clumsy foal in the pale February sunlight.

For the next five weeks I worked in the galley, my hated fore-and-aft uniform becoming greasier and greasier. My colleagues were four WRENS, René, Joyce, Black Bess and Bambi, all of whom immediately accepted me as one of the girls. Together we mopped and squeegeed the concrete floor; we were meant to call it the deck but never did so; peeled mountains of potatoes, sliced the huge grey loaves of bread, and loaded and unloaded the washing-up machine, which smelt of babies' nappies. I soon learnt to ignore the sudden clockwork-like emergence of one or more of the enormous cockroaches who lived behind it. We also did a lot of skiving and sat for hours at a time drinking ki (naval cocoa) and smoking like chimneys. I was rivetted by the erotic adventures of René, Joyce and Black Bess, which they described with a remarkable lack of inhibition. Bambi, although by far the prettiest, contributed nothing to these revelations beyond an occasional 'That'd be telling' or 'Wouldn't you like to know', and then only when pressed by the others. I suspected that, while without censoriousness, she was saving herself for Lieutenant Right.

From the rest of the ship's company, the stokers, electricians and sickberth attendants, I learnt several dodges unknown to the transient trainees. By applying to attend the Methodist Chapel in Wetherby, for example, it was possible to dive smartly down a side alley while the rest of the column marched up a certain narrow street and to spend the Godbothering hour in the back room of a friendly pub, rejoining the genuine Nonconformists at the same point during their march back to camp.

I finally made it with one of the stokers, and wrote to tell Percy at his new posting in Colombo. I often wondered if he knew what I was on about. On account of the censors I felt obliged to be what was perhaps impenetrably oblique.

When my transfer came through, a very nice Leading Seaman, who had been responsible for the discipline in my class during my abortive attempts to become a writer, invited me to join the local batch of successful trainees for a final piss-up in a country pub. We got very drunk and all I can remember of the evening was a chill but brilliant sunset lighting up a stained-glass window let into the pub door. It represented a fox holding a fat goose in its mouth. How I got back to camp I can't imagine, but the next day, with a formidable hangover but otherwise extremely happy, I set off again for Skegness.

Chapter 4

To return seven months later to Skegness was like one of those recurring dreams in which the details are a little different. I knew my way around this time but I still had to move, like a somnambulist, through the same routine: same films on VD and the correct way to brush the teeth, same elementary drill and seamanship. God remained, according to the same chaplain, the highest officer in the British Navy. Yet there were changes too. Although the war was still on, its successful conclusion, in Europe at any rate, was only a matter of time. They'd cleared the barbed wire from along the front and were digging out the anti-tank traps on the beach. They'd even re-opened the small funfair; the proud shabby horses revolved on the merry-go-round for the first time since 1939. The ghost trains banged through the double doors into an innocent world of shrieks and spectres. Back in my bellbottoms I felt reborn.

It was spring by now. I lay on the grass smoking, reading or staring up at the blue sky. The goldfish gleamed among the reeds of Billy Butlin's neglected boating-lake. The sea's horizon no longer held its threat.

In the newspapers and on the newsreel in the cinema where I went to see James Cagney in *The Roaring Twenties*, they showed us for the first time the appalling images of Belsen: the stumbling living skeletons with their bald heads and huge empty eyes, the bulldozers scooping up the mounds of dead. As far as I can remember, they hardly affected me, seeming no more real than the briefly illuminated bug-a-boos in the Skegness ghost train. How could I weep over a poem and remain indifferent to this proof of what humanity is capable of? I am unable to answer. In this respect the nineteen-year-old self that I am trying to recreate or understand is a total and repellent stranger. What did he feel as the camera explored the gas-chambers and the ovens? I can't remember. I'd like to think it was too horrible to grasp, but fear that it may be simply because I can't face up to my own self-centred lack of imagination. I wrote home praising *The Roaring Twenties*. As usual, I also asked for a small sum of money on some rather flimsy pretext. Waiting for my draft, this time to another Butlin's camp in Pwllheli, North Wales, I was given a stick with a nail in the end of it for collecting waste-paper.

I'd made a new friend, this time of undeniably working-class origin. His name was Tom Dash and, although he was a grammar school scholarship boy, his father was a dustman who lived in a pre-fab in Dalston. 'My old man's a dustman,' Tom sang in an exaggerated Cockney accent. ''E wears a dustman's 'at!' Writing to my mother I suppressed the scholarship but empha- sized his father's profession. 'He's very clever though,' I added, 'and is teaching me about a political theory called Anarchism which I find very convincing.' I knew how to tease my mother.

Actually I did find Anarchism convincing, or at any rate in so far as I was able to concentrate on the pamphlets published by Freedom Press which Tom had lent me. One of them, I was delighted to discover, was by Herbert Read, who had also edited the Faber Surrealist anthology I had found by chance in a Liverpool bookshop during the school holidays some three years earlier and carried with me everywhere since. Already believing myself a Surrealist I could now, without fear of being labelled inconsistent, declare myself an Anarchist as well. Tom saw no reason to return the compliment. His Anarchism was less romantic, based on his hatred of class oppression, on his memories as a child of Mosley's march through the East End (he had no trouble in reacting to Belsen). He found Surrealism irrelevant to the struggle, even suspect.

After the relaxed atmosphere of Skegness, HMS *Glendower* came as a nasty shock. For the first three weeks, it rained and drizzled non-stop and this coincided with more bullshit, discipline and physical unpleasantness than I had yet encountered. We had to get up at 6.30 a.m., go everywhere at the double, and perform such dangerous feats as clambering up the sixty-foot mainmast erected by the swimming-pool and climbing hand over hand upside down along a rope suspended unpleasantly high from the ground. Bellbottoms or no, there were times when I almost regretted my inability to add up and envied Percy and Harry sitting in their nice offices filling in ledgers. Falling into my bunk each night, aching all over and completely exhausted, it seemed only about ten minutes before they woke us up again. There was no shore-leave either. No time to read or think.

What they were doing, or course, was breaking us down as individuals in preparation for turning us into sailors. What I tended to forget was that my fellow sufferers had only been in the Navy for a week or two. I'd been spoilt, softened by months of cushiness and tolerated skiving.

Then, quite suddenly, things improved. We got up an hour later, the dawn was getting earlier too. The sun shone and across the parade ground Snowdon, until then invisible, rose snow-capped into the sweet spring air. I felt fitter than I ever have before or since, and mentally buzzing with new ideas as yet only partially formulated. Anarchism for instance. What a beautiful concept! A rational world in which what you made was for use not profit, and all you took was what you needed. Love was the only law. Money unnecessary. Crime, once envy, greed, and private possessions no longer existed, would be unnecessary. Why steal when you could take freely? Free sexuality would extinguish jealousy. Nobody would mind who their father was because children would be the beloved responsibility of all. War would be unthinkable; police, spies, informers, politicians redundant. It was simply a question of convincing enough people that they held the power to free themselves from their chains. They must be taught – no, persuaded – that it was useless over-turning one political system simply to embrace another. Communism, Tom had pointed out, was simply one more form of tyranny. Until then I hadn't realized this. As Communism was one of the several subjects which brought my hated prep-school headmaster to the edge of apoplexy, I thought it must be defensible. Not so, said Tom. Marx might have claimed that the end-product of Communism was the withering away of the State but the reverse was true. He gave me *Darkness at Noon* to read, and Orwell's *Homage to Catalonia*. I found them much easier to grasp than the political pamphlets, and took his point. Long live Anarchism! Down with the State!

Surrealism also. Perhaps Tom was right to reject it personally. After all there would be a lot of spade work necessary to dis-mantle the apparatus of power, to help the Workers' Syndicates supplant the bosses, to distribute food and raw materials, but at the same time purely practical activities were not enough. 'Change life,' the Surrealists had ordained. 'Tell your children your dreams!' From the few texts I'd read, from the repro-ductions of Ernst, Dali and Magritte I'd studied, I had derived amazing certainty that the marvellous was all about us, that if only we could escape from that mental labyrinth built in the name of morality, religion, patriotism and the family, we could all become poets, move through a universe where dream and reality were indistinguishable. If Anarchism was to provide the sustaining bread of life, Surrealism would pour out the intoxi-cating wine.

All this filled my head as we learnt how to clean a rifle, knelt at Church parade, or saluted the Quarter Deck, and it never occurred to me to translate my revolutionary fervour into practice through some act of refusal or defiance. I had only to shout a blasphemy in Church, refuse to salute the Quarter Deck, or throw down my rifle to prove that the status quo was as determined to protect itself as Tom maintained. I did no such thing, and nor did he, but as we argued and theorized, a true anarcho-surrealist was about to leave Skegness to join us. I knew him too. He had been at Stowe with me. His name was Tony Harris Reed.

Tony had already played a formative role in my life. Thin and almost colourless in physical appearance, he had the questing expression of a hungry ferret and, ferret-like, was prepared to track down an idea through the most complicated system of burrows. Nor was he against sinking his teeth through to the bone of the hand of anyone in authority foolish enough to try and handle him after his re-emergence. A true black humorist, he would carry a dislike to extreme ends, in no way disdaining so childish a ploy as letting down a hated master's bicycle tyres, and yet at the same time using his considerable inventive powers to build up such an exaggerated picture of the man's minor eccentricities as to reduce us all to mocking laughter at the very mention of his name.

One of his butts, an admittedly pompous history tutor, but in every other respect comparatively harmless, reduced Tony to a state of near hysterical rage, and was metamorphosed into a figure of Ubu-like proportions. The unfortunate man had a very dark, ruddy complexion which contrasted startlingly with his cropped snow-white hair and neat moustache. Tony decided he looked like the negative of a photograph. He also put it about on no evidence at all that his wife, a plain lady of no doubt entirely conventional morals, was not only an insatiable nymphomaniac but a thief to boot. In support of the latter theory he claimed that, following her by chance along an obscure path from the school's wartime fuel supply to the married masters' houses, he had at first thought her to be pregnant – no doubt the work of some precocious sixth-former or a randy if indiscriminate junior-master – but then noticed how, every now and then, a piece of coal would fall from under her bulging mackintosh. During our readings from a translation of Plato, Tony, while remaining completely po-faced himself, would imitate quite blatantly the man's affectedly clipped drawl, reducing the rest of us to ill-suppressed handkerchief-in-mouth splutterings.

He'd also cultivated a vendetta with the President of the Debating Society, a maths master of superficially liberal principles as long as everything that was said remained within certain limits. Noticing that the American popular singer, Frank Crumit, had died at an advanced age I proposed, and Tony seconded, that in future the President should wear *in perpetuum* a black tie in his memory. The master claiming, quite correctly, to fail to see any relevance in our motion refused, but was voted down by a carefully canvassed majority. From then on, whenever he failed to observe the rule, Tony or I would jump up to protest vigorously during 'any other business'.

The main target for his anarchic disrespect was less expected. It was a Canadian couple called Robin and Dodie Watt who ran the art school, a modern concrete building behind the chapel, a refuge where anybody during their spare time could go and paint or argue, a haven for generations of Stoic aesthetes and for unconventional masters as well.

Robin Watt was a quiet man who painted portraits in the style of a less exuberant Augustus John. His wife Dodie was a far more positive character. She drew well, was both kind and protective to her protégés, and managed to stimulate a great deal of interest and excitement in art in general and certain aspects of modernism in particular. She had however certain very defined ideas about what was and what wasn't acceptable in painting and, to make sure we all toed the line, would pin up paired reproductions which we were expected to divide into good, bad, or in some cases of equal merit. For example, a Matisse was 'good', a Holman Hunt was 'bad', but apples by Cézanne and Courbet were both 'good'. If we went wrong she'd explain why and, as she talked well, it proved an extremely effective form of visual brainwashing.

Arriving at Stowe, rather apprehensive, and feeling both

provincial and lost, I found the Watts and their art school an unexpected haven, and was soon preaching their gospel during the holidays not only to my mother and small sister but also to my various Liverpudlian relations, including a rich cousin of my grandfather's, who took it pretty well considering that my lecture took place in a large drawing-room hung with original pre-Raphaelites collected by her father, a nineteenth-century ship-owner.

At first Harris Reed was equally under the spell of Robin and Dodie Watt. Indeed he produced with remarkable facility a huge number of precocious pictures in the style of those painters we were taught to admire. Yellow crucifixions against pink land-scapes in the manner of early Gauguin yielded to cubist still-lives on up-tilted table-tops after Braque. Matisse nudes jostled Chagall lovers. Picasso harlequins sat amidst Derainesque land-scapes. The rest of us were dazzled by his eclectic brilliance although the Watts, while by no means wishing to discourage so receptive a disciple, felt he ought to spend a little more time improving his rather shaky draftsmanship.

Given that Ma and Pa Watt, as we had come to call them, were our father and mother figures, there came that inevitable moment during our later adolescence when we began to question their authority, and here Tony turned what might otherwise have been little more than a series of mild disagreements on the relative importance of this or that painter into a full-scale revolt.

It was my discovery of Herbert Read's book on Surrealism which acted as the catalyst. I'd brought it back to school in a state of high excitement and carried it, like a trusting puppy, to the Watts for their approval. They were of course both aware of Surrealism, having visited that pre-war exhibition in London which had led to the publication of Read's anthology in the first place. Furthermore, in the art school library was a copy of E. L. T. Mesens' *London Bulletin – No 1* which contained a reproduction of Magritte's *Le Viol* which Ma and Pa Watt dismissed as sensationalism and, more damagingly, 'literary', although personally and secretly I'd found it both disturbing and impressive.

It was a weekly custom of the Watts to hold, in their own room, a discussion-meeting-cum-sketch-club and it was here I produced my book. There were about eight of us there, including Tony and Guy Neal, the third member of our little clique. It was Guy who'd first introduced me to jazz. I'd shown both Tony and Guy the book earlier, and they had shared my enthusiasm. Ma Watt looked rapidly through the reproductions, screwing up her eyes behind her glasses as was her habit. She was almost entirely dismissive. 'Old hat' was her first condemnation of the movement as a whole. She was willing to allow that Klee, Miro and of course Picasso were OK, but dismissed Dali, Magritte and Ernst as 'no damn good'. Robin mumbled his agreement. I felt very depressed, but then, in an unprecedented way, Tony and Guy began to argue quite forcefully. Ma Watt stood her ground. 'Silly Freudian images painted as photographically and as badly as the Pre-Raphaelites.' Taking courage from my bolder friends, I too began to question the whole aesthetic grid through which Ma Watt judged pictures and the meeting, usually so civilized, finished on quite a sour note. The following week, despite considerable grumpiness from both Ma and Pa Watt as to the value of what we were doing, Tony, Guy and I began to turn out pictures in the orthodox Surrealist manner.

Tony didn't let things rest there, however. Taking advantage of Ma Watt's absence (I believe she suffered from migraines), he asked the more easily persuaded Robin if we could use the small sculpture room for a Surrealist exhibition. He tentatively agreed, thinking that we intended to do no more than hang up our pictures. Not so. The following Thursday, the Watts' day off, we set to work with full iconoclastic enthusiasm. We jammed a large doll's head over the taps of the sink so that the water poured out of its neck on to a piece of coral. We smashed in the breasts of a classical plaster-cast bust and put tins of condensed milk in the cavities. We dragged in a dustbin and filled it with the dismembered limbs of the school's skeleton, painted shocking pink. We scattered dead leaves all over the floor. We hung our pictures too of course, but copied out various Surrealist texts below and above them in poster paint. We also imported two or three gramophones and attached various incongruous objects from the still-life cupboard to their slowly revolving turntables. We were rather pleased with the general effect.

Next day we hid behind a low cupboard on all fours waiting for the Watts to arrive. Unfortunately, believing the art school to be empty, Ma Watt allowed herself the luxury of a discreet fart and Pa Watt, following in her wake, asked if she'd 'pooped'. This set us off into audible giggles. Ma Watt ordered us out from behind the cupboard, told us off for being childish, and asked us suspiciously why we were hiding there anyway. We told her we wanted to hear her reaction to our Surrealist exhibition without her feeling inhibited. 'What Surrealist exhibition?' she snapped. Her husband explained that he'd said we could hang our pictures in the sculpture room.

Snorting with irritation at his compliance, she threw open the door. We needn't have shown any fear as to the inhibition of her reactions. She went puce with rage, told us to clear up 'that damn insulting *mess*!' and barred us from the art school for a week. Tony was delighted. We'd *proved* her bourgeois conformism masquerading as tolerant modernity. It was up to us now not to go crawling back. We didn't show up for the rest of the term. I decorated my study with the bust with the condensed milk-tin breasts and we met there to play our jazz records – Ma Watt had objected to the seriousness we'd showed in that area too. 'It's just fun music,' she'd complained.

Eventually Guy and I made it up with the Watts, but Tony Harris Reed never did. I looked forward to his arrival at Pwllheli with rather anxious anticipation.

At first sight, but this was not unexpected, Tony looked un-exceptional. His uniform fitted him, his hat was on at the pre-scribed angle. He hadn't even bothered to bleach his collar. I introduced him to Tom and the rest of my circle of friends. He and Tom didn't really take to each other. Tom's idealism, which had, during the past few weeks, coloured my own thought-patterns, seemed rather wet to Tony's way of thinking. *His* anarchism was more mocking and subversive. He had little belief in the effectiveness of political or anti-political action. On the other hand, since I had last seen him, he had rooted out a great deal more information about Surrealism, discovering for example that there was an active group in London led by the Belgian poet and collagist E. L. T. Mesens, then 42, the friend and entrepreneur of Magritte, and the publisher of the pre-war *London Bulletin*. In the back of the *New Statesman* he had found an advertisement for several recently published pamphlets and broadsheets, as well as a book of Mesens' own poetry and another by Paul Eluard, translated by someone called Roland Penrose. Tony had some money and I, as usual, wrote home for some, and we sent off for these in high anticipation.

Meanwhile, under Tony's sharp eye, life at HMS *Glendower* began to assume a more hallucinatory aspect. He was quick to recognize the potential, as 'a surreal personage', of a boy I introduced him to with the curious name of Arding Jones, and it was he, rather than Tom, who became an intimate.

Arding Jones was as odd as his name. He was tall, hawk-like and with a really depressing acne-scarred skin. He'd been to public school and was superficially a traditional rugger-bugger, but he fancied only pretty working-class lads. To make his life more difficult, however, he was reduced to a ferocious rage by working-class accents irrespective of their region of origin, a dilemma he solved by taking out his fancy and spending a great deal of money on the pictures, beer, the cinema, etc, *on condition the boy didn't open his mouth once.* Stranger still, he was never without a companion usually, to me, most enviably desirable. I had found this rather shocking, although I liked Arding well enough, but Tony relished the absurdity of it. The long silent evenings, full of loving glances, but with no verbal communication, he said, must be intensely erotic.

Among Arding's other peculiarities was his insistence on masturbating twice a day at exactly 11 a.m. and 3 p.m. (or 1500 hours as the Navy insisted we call it). As a rule this presented little difficulty. If we were in class studying gunnery or semaphor signals, he would simply ask to go to 'the heads'.

Occasionally however there would arise a situation which presented what one might imagine to be a more tricky problem. One morning we were all detailed off to help a local farmer thin out some root crop, and 10.45 a.m. found us isolated in the centre of an enormous field with another hour and a half to go before the lunch break. Amused expectations arose, for everybody knew of Arding's clocking-in time. At 11 a.m. precisely, he left the furrow, marched smartly a distance of some ten yards, lay down, undid the flap on the front of his working bellbottoms, and set to entirely uninhibited by our noisy encouragement, and appearing in no way disconcerted by our ironic applause at his success.

The final, and in some ways most unlikely, facet of Arding's character was a fierce republicanism. This was in no way unsympathetic to me, as a Surrealist and an anarchist: the centrist argument that a monarch, above parliamentary or political affiliations, was the best defence against totalitarianism naturally held no weight. Even so Arding's ferocity, bordering on mania, astonished me. He wouldn't even refer to the King by name; he called him 'Korky the King', a form of alliteration he'd based on 'Korky the Kat', a character in the *Dandy* comic. In particular his subterfuges to avoid standing for the National Anthem, except when completely unavoidable as on the parade ground, went to any lengths and he would sooner miss the last five minutes of a film than remain at attention during what he always called 'Korky's tune'. Sometimes we were caught out; a film came to an end without the usual slow fade-out or give-away swelling chords, but even then he would rush agitatedly up the aisle muttering angry runes and imprecations like a vampire confronted with a crucifix. I felt obliged in his company to follow and, indeed, one night we ran into the erect form of a Warrant Officer who took our names and numbers, and we were reported and given three days' 'number elevens', that is to say, confined to camp and put through an hour of punitive drill to boot. Arding was in no way contrite. He blamed it all on Korky.

Arding liked neither jazz nor Surrealism, but he, Tony

and I spent a lot of time ashore together. Not that I deserted Tom. I went ashore with him too, but had to admit to myself that our evenings together lacked something of the hysterical and mythical quality of my nights with Arding and Tony.

Tony in his own right had begun to operate effectually. Strengthened by the Surrealist canon, for the books had arrived and we spent many hours absorbing their message, we both declared ourselves convinced atheists, and Tony's first practical demonstration of our new-found freedom from 'Judeo-Christian mysticism' was to steal some bottles of admittedly unconsecrated Communion wine from the chapel, and we all got extremely and indeed disastrously drunk in his chalet.

We had also decided that we should write to Mesens in London pledging our fealty to Surrealism, and, to this end, Tony began to make some beautiful if excessively Ernst-influenced collages – I remember one in which some Victorian sportsmen were engaged in shooting at a flying turtle – while I had begun to write poetry of what I hoped was a genuinely Surrealist flavour. 'The egg is always surrounded by birds,' one of my poems concluded. 'The gun by corpses, the bicycle by lovers/We are going to ascend in this ornate balloon/Much to the astonishment of the ladies and gents.'

When we had created enough collages and poems, we sent them off to the address printed on the Surrealist pamphlets and waited anxiously for a reply.

Meanwhile we strove, within the limits imposed by the Navy, to live the Surrealist life. There was, for example, the visit to the Abyssinian princesses. Rumours reached us from one of Arding's lads (for there was no embargo on them speaking to us when he himself wasn't within earshot) that in the nearby village of Criccieth, three young 'darkies' had been sighted riding their bicycles through the chapel-haunted streets. This in itself excited me. Through jazz anyone black had become sacred and I was always writing home to tell my mother that I would only marry a negress, and that there was no question that if Bessie Smith had still been alive it would have been her. (How the

Empress of the Blues would have reacted to my proposal never occurred to me then.)

A little later I found out something more concrete about the three girls. They were grand-daughters of the 'Lion of Judah', and this, as I explained to Tony Harris Reed, gave me an entrée. My father's cousin, John Melly, a witty life-loving man of strong Christian principles, had taken out, in his capacity as a doctor, the only British ambulance team during the Abyssinian war. He had unfortunately been killed on the very last day, shot by a drunken Ethiopian who'd mistaken him for an Italian, but he was considered to be a great hero by both the Emperor and his people. (There is a John Melly Street in Addis Ababa and a wing of the hospital is named after him.) We had, therefore, every excuse to call on the Lion's grand-cubs. I proposed that it would be truly 'Surreal' to visit them in a Welsh village wearing our best bellbottoms. Tony agreed, and, on the next make-and-mend, we walked between the lush Welsh summer hedges to the little town and, after a couple of enquiries from extremely voluble locals, found our way to their modest lodgings.

A suspicious Welsh landlady with a small but definitive beard answered the door and, after listening to our explanation, showed us reluctantly into a small parlour while she went off to fetch the princesses' governess. It was a very Welsh parlour, hung with admonishing texts promising a far from reassuring future life. There was a table in the window with a potted fern on its dark-green bobble-edged cloth and many faded sepia photographs of the dead. What undid us though was a large Victorian steel engraving above the mantelshelf. It showed a small child wearing a nightgown and in the act of embracing a presumably symbolic sheep. The sheep in its turn regarded the child with what I presume the artist intended to be an expression of loving anthropomorphic piety but, to our eyes, it seemed almost grotesquely lascivious while at the same time extremely shifty. We began to giggle, and the sudden entrance of landlady and governess discovered us almost helpless with hysterical laughter. This made our task the harder. The governess was Scottish, with pale ginger hair and a forbidding expression, but we managed eventually to persuade her that I had a genuine reason for meeting her charges, and we were asked reluctantly to stay to tea.

This in fact proved quite a success. The princesses were very beautiful, their glowing black skins and fine features appearing doubly exotic in the dusty little diningroom, with its ticking marble clock. They were also full of high spirits and Tony and I made them laugh a great deal so that even the governess allowed herself an occasional frosty smile. Indeed one joke led to a minor disaster. Princess Ruth, the youngest, had just swallowed a mouthful of orangeade when something Tony said caught her unawares and she performed the nose-trick.

'Dearie me!' said the governess, busy with a handkerchief. 'Poor Princess Ruth has been quite overcome!'

Our training continued, but became a little easier. On the cliffs at the edge of the camp we learnt to fire a mounted anti-aircraft machine-gun. Our instructor was a short and tubby Geordie Petty Officer who demonstrated the effectiveness of the weapon with a certain practical ferocity.

'Yer see that shite-hawk,' he said, pointing to a lone seagull flying from left to right across the middle distance. We agreed we did. He fired a short burst.

'Well now yer doant!' he told us with savage satisfaction. Tony and I wondered how many innocent shite-hawks had involuntarily sacrificed their lives in this way in the service of democracy.

One day, the war in Europe was over. It wasn't a night we were due to go ashore, nor was it an occasion I can especially remember. Everybody got rather drunk. Some chalet windows were broken and a few wire litter baskets set on fire. Next day training continued as usual. There was still the Japanese. The arrest of the chief Nazis, the discovery of the charred bodies of Hitler and Eva Braun in the Berlin bunker, seemed almost a logical and commonplace conclusion to the whole phantasmagoria. Tony and I felt more concerned about waiting to hear from the Surrealists in London.

We had meanwhile acquired an enemy, a Warrant Officer, the same man who had apprehended Arding and myself leaving the cinema during the National Anthem. He, disliking our levity, our background, and our rather flirtatious relationship with the Petty Officers, did what he could to harass us. One day Tony devised a very typical revenge.

We had found on the shore during our long and excitable walks in pursuit of the 'marvellous', a large dead starfish and brought it back to camp. Then one of us put forward an idea for a Surrealist object. We would buy a common mousetrap and put the starfish in it as though it had been caught. This we did and so pleased were we with the effect that we decided to take it into Pwllheli and have it photographed, intending, if the result was satisfactory, to send a print to London in pursuit of the poems and collages and in the hope of expediting our yearned-for acknowledgment. Tony decided, however, that we could draw a subtle advantage from this activity. After making sure our enemy, the Warrant Officer, was to inspect the Liberty Men, he placed the object in an empty tickler tin and persuaded me to conceal it in my mackintosh pocket in so furtive and yet obvious a way as to lead to certain detection.

'Tickler' is naval slang for duty-free tobacco and in those days every rating was entitled at regular intervals to a large tin, at an extremely modest price. This was a great help financially but naturally enough, given the rarity of cigarettes in 'Civvy Street', there was a considerable temptation to smuggle one's ration ashore in order to sell it at an enormous profit, and to help dissuade us from this course the penalties, if caught, were correspondingly severe.

Tony knew that our enemy, the Warrant Officer, who always inspected us with particular thoroughness, would be sure to find the tin, and so he did.

'What have you got in that pocket, Seaman?'

'A tickler tin, sir.'

A grim smile of satisfaction spread across his face as he told me to pull it out. The rest of the Liberty Men were torn between resentment at being held up and pleasure in the discomfort of a fellow rating. Making much of it, I finally and apparently reluctantly pulled the tin out of my pocket. He asked me, very sarcastically, what was in it. I told him the exact truth – a starfish caught in a mousetrap. A wild incredulous whoop of laughter rose from those near enough to hear my answer. It was relayed in whispers to those further down the ranks. Our enemy turned extremely red. He took the tin and opened it. He extracted our object. He looked at it, replaced it, and handed me back the tin. He next asked me why I was taking it out of the camp. 'To have it photographed, sir,' I explained. More laughter. He ordered silence, completed his inspection and let us march ashore. Tony and I were cock-a-hoop. Our cruelty caused us not a moment's pause. Like school-masters, Warrant Officers were fair game. The photographs were unsuccessful; the local photographer, usually confined to the recording of weddings, funerals and Eisteddfods, was unwilling to accept the commission in the first place and the result, after we talked him into it, reflected his suspicious bewilderment.

At long last a short letter arrived for us from the Surrealist Group in London. It expressed interest if no great enthusiasm for our work, and suggested that if either of us were in London in the future, we should contact the secretary, Simon Watson Taylor, at a Chelsea address. We were a little disappointed. We'd both hoped to receive something more positive, and we were depressed too that the letter was signed only by the secretary to the group, and not by E. L. T. Mesens himself. Still at least we'd heard, at least we had an entrée.

Shortly afterwards we passed out as Ordinary Seamen, and after a few weeks hanging about as officers' messengers, or Quartermasters' mates, we were sent home on a fortnight's leave. Tony, a Portsmouth rating alas, would then report to his home barracks, I to Chatham, a town I knew to be intoxicatingly close to London. I only hoped I would be stationed there long enough to make at least some initial contact with the Surrealist Group.

Chapter 5

I arrived at Chatham barracks on a dank July evening. My hammock and kitbag weighed me down and I had bad dhoby itch as well. Dhoby itch is a weeping rash in the crutch caused by failing to rinse the suds out from one's underpants. It is a most dispiriting complaint.

I reported to the Petty Officer on duty. He told me the barracks were full and that I was to sleep on HMS *Argus*, a superannuated aircraft carrier rusting away in the dockyards adjoining the barracks, and which was in use an as overflow base. 'Don't bother to make yourself cushy though,' he advised me with a wolfish smile. 'We'll 'ave you out East before the fuckin' week's out.'

I tried to appear enthusiastic at this prospect, picked up my hammock and kitbag again, and walked bow-legged and in some discomfort through the dockyard gates in the direction indicated. Twenty breathless and sweaty minutes later I found the *Argus* looming up into the darkening drizzle, and staggered up the gangway on to the quarter deck. Formalities completed, I was shown my mess deck, and later, after a revolting supper of what appeared to be camel's entrails, slung my hammock for the first time. Bearing in mind what the Petty Officer had promised, I left my kitbag unpacked. After a few days of digging about in it to find things I needed, I slowly transferred its contents to my locker. I was to remain on HMS *Argus* for over a year.

The *Argus*, as I soon discovered, was a den of skivers, misfits and lunatics, a floating, tethered thieves' kitchen. Our Captain, an elderly and scrawny religious maniac risen from the ranks, seldom left his cabin and could be heard, during the night watches, loudly declaiming the more bloodthirsty passages from the Old Testament. Despite his age and length of service, he was still, and understandably, a Lieutenant. The rest of the ship's company were all involved in a conspiracy to remain exactly where they were, tucked snugly away, a cosy and corrupt community dedicated to mutual aid. Among them I soon became friendly with an open-faced and charming rogue nicknamed Wings and after a short time I became his official winger. The expression 'winger' means, at its most innocent, a young seaman who is taken under the wing of a rating or Petty Officer older and more experienced than himself to be shown the ropes. It can also, although far from inevitably, imply a homosexual relationship, and in our case this was so, but on a comparatively playful and lighthearted level, mostly confined to rum-flavoured kisses when he returned on board.

Wings filled me in on many useful dodges. For example he advised me never to attend the regular pay parades in the barracks. At these parades suspicious marines stalked about seeking out ratings who might be posted to ships about to sail East. Far better to attend the miss-musters parade when those who had been on watch duty drew their money, and only a bored officer and an equally indifferent Petty Officer were present.

To ensure this end he advised me to land a watchkeeping job

and I soon managed it. A friendly Chief Petty Officer made me a boatswain's mate. This proved to be chilly and monotonous; twenty-four hours on duty; four hours watch and watch about on the open quarter deck, checking the leave passes of ratings going on or coming off leave and saluting, and occasionally physically assisting aboard, the officers. The advantage was that after coming off duty I was entitled to forty-eight hours shore leave, quite long enough to get up to London, and that every other weekend there was seventy-eight hours off, time enough for me to get up to Liverpool.

Wings had advice here too. As to London he suggested that, if I decided I had a future as 'rough trade', I should haunt either a pub in Victoria or another in Piccadilly. He himself had been successful in both of them. He told me that if picked up by an old queen who, in the morning, turned out to be less than generous, he usually knocked them about a bit and then walked off with whatever he fancied. He insisted that it was common practice and furthermore it was his view that 'most of the old buggers' expected it or even enjoyed it. I was really shocked at Wings and did not believe him, or at any rate chose not to. In another branch of petty criminal activity, however, he was to prove extremely helpful.

Getting to London presented no difficulty; it was quite cheap by train or you could hitch-hike. On the other hand, a return ticket to Liverpool was comparatively expensive and, with only four free travel warrants a year, it looked as though I should, yet again, have to cadge off my parents. 'No need,' said Wings when I had explained my dilemma, and he demonstrated an ingenious method whereby, with the aid of a local return ticket, ink remover, diluted Stephen's green ink, and some reliance on the dim lighting at station barriers and the senility of the wartime inspectors, you could get to any major provincial station and back for approximately five shillings. I practised this deception many times during my *Argus* period. So did many of my fellow ratings, but as far as I can remember no one was ever caught out.

You might wonder why, with London so close and ready to be explored and conquered, I should wish to return to Liverpool at all except for long leaves. The answer was that, while certain that in the end I would become the toast of the town, I realized it might take a little time and meanwhile it was a solace to be able to return home where my mother's unfailing belief in my eventual triumph, the comfort of friends, the admiration of my twelve-year-old sister, and, above all, the familiar port heavy with childhood associations would help to restore my confidence. To be frank I was a little in awe of London; a state fostered equally by my father's reluctance to visit it except when his business as a woolbroker had positively demanded it, and my mother's pre-war expeditions which, on her return, loaded with toys from Hamley's, she painted in the most brilliant of colours. 'I did eight shows in six days,' she'd tell us excitedly, 'and went three times to the Savoy Grill with Rex Evans [a night-club owner and performer of the period] and had lunch at the Ivy twice with dear Bobby.' It sounded rather formidably sophisticated. Also, everytime we went to our dentist, a Mr Williams, who had his surgery, like many of the medical profession in Liverpool, in Rodney Street, a rather beautiful Georgian terrace, she would say that they were 'just like London houses'. Sitting tipped back in Mr Williams' dentist chair, while he chattered to my mother about the latest production at the Playhouse and did painful things inside my mouth, I would imagine that the sky over London must look much as it did above the opposite side of the street and, as I was to recognize much later, the word 'London' had become subconsciously associated, and a little anxiously, with dentistry.

It was, therefore, with a certain tentative apprehension that I began to explore the metropolis. It was true that I had visited it once before. When I was ten, Emma Holt, a rich and kindly cousin of my grandfather's, had offered us a choice: she would either pay for my father to take my brother and me up to watch King George VI's coronation procession from a balcony in the Mall or, if we would prefer it, we could spend a whole week in the capital later in that same year. After some debate we chose the latter, stayed with an aunt in a flat overlooking the river at Barnes and exhausted my poor father by racing round the zoo,

Madame Tussaud's, the Tower and other traditional 'sights'. There was however little to compare between this protected and sponsored expedition as a child and my return, almost nine years later, as a solitary seaman. It's true that there were relations of my mother's living in flats, mainly in genteelly unfashionable areas, and friends of hers too with more central addresses and connected with the arts, but obstinately, before contacting anybody, even the Surrealists, I wanted to get at least the feel of the place, to establish at any rate the broadest outline of its central geography, and so for the first month I did little more than walk the streets, visit the museums or, getting on a tube train, travel at random, emerging from any station familiar by name, usually because it figured in 'Monopoly'.

I also tried to follow Wings' example (we never went 'up the smoke' together, as for one thing he was on the opposite watch from me and, for another, he considered, quite rightly, that my middle-class effeminacy would reduce his impact as rough trade). Perhaps for this very reason I was not a success with the corsetted and discreetly rouged old gentlemen who combed the gay pubs. Occasionally one of them would offer me a half of Guinness, but he would soon lose interest and move towards a more masculine fellow seaman or haughty guardsman, leaving me to my *New Statesman* at the marble-topped bar. While rather hurt, I was not entirely unrelieved either. The point was that, while coming on as what Bessie Smith called 'a skippin' twistin' woman-actin' man,' my real taste was also for butch young men, but with myself in the masculine role. Much later a perceptive if rather coarse-minded rating expressed this with obscenely poetic exactitude: 'You're not a brown 'atter at all,' he said. 'You're an arse-bandit what acts like 'e was a brown 'atter!'

One night, it's true, I did make a conquest. Having forgotten to book in at the Union Jack Club (1/6d a night), I was sitting shivering in a seat in Leicester Square when a small, middle-aged, respectable-looking man wearing glasses and a Crombie overcoat approached me. After offering me a cigarette, he followed it up with a sofa, which I accepted, in his flat in Dolphin Square. I wasn't deceived by the sofa and was glad to be warm and comfortable, but wished he had not brushed his teeth so thoroughly as the taste of Gibb's Dentrifrice was overwhelming. At breakfast in the dining room next morning, for I was on a forty-eight hour pass, I had the mild jitters as I knew that somewhere in that huge 1930 rabbit warren of flats there lived a great friend of my mother's, an elderly and obsessively respectable actress who would certainly feel it her duty to report back. That morning, however, she must have taken her breakfast in her flat (Meissen figurines and old playbills), and I left fed and rested for the Victoria and Albert Museum. My closet queen made no effort to arrange another meeting, nor did he offer me 'a present'. I was clearly a final resort; a sheep in wolf's clothing. He would have much preferred Wings and his ilk. For my part I looked speculatively round his flat. What would Wings have taken? The ivory-handled hairbrush? The heavy 'portable' wireless? It was purely academic. The idea of threatening someone of approximately my own class and who, that toothpaste flavoured half-hour apart, had behaved like a kindly if boring uncle or friendly housemaster was out of the question.

Once I'd established what I thought of as 'the magic square', that is to say the relative position of Regent Street, Oxford Street, Park Lane and Piccadilly, I felt secure enough to begin to ring people up. At first it was cousins of my mother; gentle middle-class, middle-aged Jewish ladies who had a spare bed or at least a sofa, but later, as the parks, Soho and Chelsea assumed their approximate location on my mental map, I took to visiting her more artistic friends: a theatrical producer with a flat on the King's Road, a butch actor, and, above all, David Webster who had just come down from Liverpool, to a chorus of vicious screeching from most of the musical establishment, to take up his position as Managing Director of Covent Garden.

I had known David since I was a little boy and like most of my mother's circle had been encouraged to call him Uncle David, a form of address which, now that I was about the same age as many of his younger friends, I was firmly forbidden to employ.

David was and always had been plump, he had gone bald early; my parents had known him from a very young man and told me that he had always looked exactly the same. He was not especially scrupulous about his person: his nails were, as my mother said, 'in mourning', his suits, while well cut, had their collars powdered with dandruff. This was of no importance, however, because he had been born almost unfairly endowed with charm and wit. In the Liverpool of the Twenties and Thirties he ruled the artistic roost. The son of small Scottish shopkeepers (and although in many ways extremely snobbish, he'd never tried to hide them away or upgrade his social origins), he soon proved himself to be brilliant in many directions and with particular flair and feeling for the arts. After graduating from Liverpool University, he'd become extremely active, directing and acting in plays. 'His feet,' said my mother describing his appearance as Becket in Eliot's *Murder in the Cathedral*, 'were none too clean.' He'd also taken part in cabarets organized by the members of The Sandon, a club connected with the arts, and here his appearance as Epstein's Genesis in labour under a green spotlight was long remembered. But it was more probably his chairmanship of the Liverpool Philharmonic which had led to his present, much questioned, position.

Unlike his parents he hadn't a trace of Scottish accent, but there was a certain precision combined with richness in his delivery which hinted at his Caledonian roots, and eliminated any possibility of a Liverpudlian background. He had, from early in his life, cultivated the friendship of artists and writers. Edith Sitwell sent him her books with warm dedications on the fly-leaf and he had a great many amusing stories to tell about his various encounters with Mrs Patrick Campbell in her later years. His house, in a Victorian suburb of Liverpool, seemed to me, as a child, the essence of sophistication. The drawing-room had a white carpet, there was a Matthew Smith still-life over the grand piano and, lounging elegantly about, beautiful young men, all of whom were creative in some way. This one played the piano, that one designed ballet sets. Outside, the sunlight itself seemed less raw, more urbane than anywhere else in Liverpool.

David, however, believed in work. He needed money to defend his life-style and was not ashamed to earn it in commerce.

To this end he had risen to become Managing Director of Bon Marché, Liverpool's most fashionable big store. I adored Bon Marché. The ground floor smelt of scent and rich furs and here too, shopping with my mother, one was most likely to come upon Uncle David sampling the home-made chocolates, for he was, it must be admitted, extremely greedy.

Both chocolates and David Webster figured in my first grown up homosexual experience. Early in the war, while still at Stowe, I had been asked to act the role of Lady Macbeth; it was to be directed by Professor G. Wilson Knight, the distinguished, if eccentric, Shakespearian scholar who was at that time one of the strangely assorted staff. I learnt the part in the holidays and, wishing to appear one-up on my return to school, asked David if he would give me some advice. He had himself directed and played Macbeth some years before, casting my mother, who was in fact rather irritated not to have played Lady Macbeth, as the third witch. Sixteen years old and alone with David in his drawing-room . . .

'I have given suck and know how sweet it is . . .'

'More passion, dear. You sound as if you are opening a garden fête. Have another chocolate.' For despite rationing, there was a big box on the low glass table and they were proper chocolates too, each in its little crinkly nest and some of them wrapped in gold paper.

Then, when we'd finished, he kissed me on the mouth. I hadn't really enjoyed it, but revelled in the idea of it. Since I was thirteen, I'd been making eyes at all my mother's friends I knew to be gay and finally one of them had responded, so I ran home to tell my ten-year-old sister. I'd already sold her the glamour of homosexuality and we'd go for long walks in the parks appraising the ragamuffins in their torn jerseys. 'How much more beautiful,' I'd say to her, 'is the word "boy" than the word "girl",' and she, flattered to receive my attention and confidences, would solemnly agree.

Now, via a wartime stint at the Ministry of Production under Sir Stafford Cripps, David had left Bon Marché for the Garden to prepare for its re-opening after its wartime metamorphosis into a dance-hall. He had moved into an impressive modern house near the BBC. The attacks on him were both underhand – 'the homosexual haberdasher' was a particularly snobbish epithet – and unrealistic. He knew, after all, a great deal about opera and ballet and he had many friends in both worlds. Furthermore, through his experience in running a big store, he had a grasp of business, of costing, of handling people in organizations, which was denied to the more obvious candidates for the job.

When I rang him the first time, he was kindness itself and immediately asked me round for a drink. I felt able from then on to call him whenever I wanted to, while at the same time aware that it would be a mistake to presume too often. Despite Lady Macbeth and the chocolates, I was not really his type. Partially to my relief, partially bruising to my vanity, he never made a pass at me again.

Chapter 6

My real reason for not contacting the Surrealist Group immediately was that I feared, as I still fear, rejection, and reading the formal, icy attacks of André Breton on those he found inadequate or hypocritical (a style of vituperation echoed in those English pamphlets which Tony and I had poured over in Pwllheli), in no way reassured me. The thing was that I believed, and to this day still tend to believe, that everybody shares my obsessions. For example, on one of my first visits to London, I had approached a policeman in Regent Street and asked him, to his justifiable astonishment, where Freddy Mirfield and his Garbage Men were playing that night. Mr Mirfield had only made one record, a rather weak approximation to Chicago jazz although in retrospect of some historical interest in that among other Garbage Men was a very young clarinettist called Johnny Dankworth. It is very likely that the band was a pick-up group, certainly they never made another record, and yet I took it for granted that because I knew about them, they would be playing every night in London at a well-known dance-hall. In the same way I visualized the Surrealists, those wizards who at any moment were about to change the world, as occupying a large headquarters hung with masterpieces, full of studios where some people painted or constructed objects and others wrote poetry of crystalline purity or issued manifestos of impeccable revolutionary fervour, and where rooms were set aside for acts of erotic delirium.

I hesitated, therefore, to ring up Simon Watson Taylor at his Flaxman number, believing that I might be found wanting immediately, denounced for wearing a uniform or unmasked as a homosexual, a deviation I gathered Breton disapproved of because of the frivolity and aesthetic freemasonry of people like Cocteau and their tendency to exploit the more superficial aspects of Surrealism for purely fashionable ends. I didn't admit to this reasoning, pretending to myself that it was important to wait until Tony Harris Reed could join me, and to this end wrote to him frequently to establish a date when he had both sufficient leave and sufficient money to make the journey up from Portsmouth. He answered non-committally but the truth was that, although later on he did meet Mesens on one occasion, his enthusiasm was already waning and he had begun to apply his sardonic concentration to another of his interests, racing. Comparatively soon, we lost touch, but I met him some years later in a pub, dressed in the loudest of checks, and earning his living as a newspaper tipster, calling himself Major in line with his profession.

In the end, therefore, I plucked up my courage and rang Simon Watson Taylor from a phone box in Chatham dockyard. He sounded polite if rather abrupt and I arranged to go to his Chelsea flat the following Saturday at midday. It was my usual custom then, if the weather was fine, to hitch-hike into London from the outskirts of Rochester. It was too unreliable a method to risk on the way back because one had to report on board at a specified time, but drivers, both commercial and civilian, were still generously disposed to picking up servicemen and it save quite a lot of money. That day, nervous but excited, clasping my ditty box, I left the dockyard and was soon sitting high up next to an old lorry driver whose false teeth were so poor a fit you could hear them forming fours above the roar of the engine. As he had to turn off towards the docks at Blackheath he dropped me at the top of the hill which falls away towards New Cross, and I stood there looking down at the bomb-scarred city below me glittering in the winter sun. In my ditty box were a bottle of ink, a pen, a grubby towel, a sponge bag and a new poem typed on a naval typewriter on pink paper. It was called 'The Heir':

> 'Naked, he makes small red tears.
> A monster (with beautiful eyes and hands),
> Who blames his father.'

I felt like a Surrealist Dick Whittington, and a little later thumbed a lift in a car which dropped me off at Charing Cross where, after a few minutes at the stop outside the anti-vivisectionists' headquarters, I caught a number eleven bus to Chelsea and rang the bell of Simon's flat in Markham Square.

Simon was a few years older than I. He was small but neatly made, full of aggressive energy fuelled by alcohol, controlled by discipline. He was dressed in a well-cut conservative tweed suit with an expensive shirt and tie. His eyes blazed with intelligence. His hair was short, cut *en brosse* by an excellent barber. His humour was icy. I found him impressive and rather intimidating. His flat, however, was something of a disappointment. There were a few etchings by Miro and Dali but little sense of fantasy and the furniture, while comfortable, was banal in the extreme. We talked for some time and in my usual, parrot-like wish to make appropriate noises, I declared my adherence to Surrealism in a solemn style deriving from the translations of Breton's ornate classic French into a rather stilted English. Simon listened to me with sardonic kindness and only when, to curry favour further, I attacked homosexuality did he correct me by saying that several of the greatest Surrealists, Crevel for a start, had been queer or at any rate bi-sexual and that it was only Breton who had found it necessary to rationalize his own feelings of repulsion towards that particular deviation. The only trouble with the human body, Simon said, was that there were not enough holes in it for the exploration of human pleasure.

I must have been maddening, but it was clear after an hour that he had taken a liking to me and a friendship was established that has lasted to this day.

It seemed to me perfectly natural that after a time he should open a cupboard on the shelves of which were neatly arranged, each in its cardboard cover, the most enormous and amazing collection of rare 78 rpm jazz and blues records including many original Bessie Smiths. As he was a Surrealist, I thought, *of course* he'd like jazz. He declared his belief in Anarchism too, and promised to introduce me to the London Anarchist Group, some of whom had only recently been released from prison for causing disaffection among the troops through their publication *Freedom*. I expressed my eagerness, but was even more excited when he suggested that I might attend the next Surrealist 'séance' the following Monday in a private dining room of the Barcelona Restaurant, Beak Street.

He had an appointment in the afternoon; somehow Simon's appointments always impressed me as very portentous and serious; but first he offered me lunch and we walked along King's Road to a rather disgusting little restaurant (even by the standards of the time) called the Bar-B-Cue where we ate Spanish omelettes under a poor mural of cowboys roping steers. I was, I must admit, in a state of delirious excitement at lunching with the secretary of the Surrealist Group in England.

In the Bar-B-Cue was an extraordinary figure, surrounded by an admiring circle of bohemians, whom we joined for coffee. 'Mr Watson Taylor,' said this person, 'sit down and tell me the story of your life, and introduce me to your friend in bell-bottoms.' It was obvious to me that as Simon, while heterosexual himself, knew this man, I had made a considerable tactical error in assuming that all the Surrealists shared Breton's mistrust of deviation. His name was Quentin Crisp and he was then I should guess in his middle thirties. Being in Chelsea he was unshaven and rather grubby, the nail varnish on both finger and toe nails, peeping through gilt sandals, cracked and flaked, his mascara in need of attention, his lipstick of renewal. He had, however, a wistful, frail beauty and a wicked wit. His hair was henna red, a common enough sight now but unseen then on ostensibly male heads. I thought him extraordinary and suspected, rightly so as it turned out, that he must have the courage of a lioness to walk the streets of London. Indeed, he was frequently insulted, sometimes assaulted and now and then was in trouble with the law, who objected, not to any overt act, for there he was very discreet, but to his appearance in general.

My equation of Chelsea with grubbiness may seem too broad a generalization, but it was exact in relation to Quentin. He lived and lives in an amazingly squalid room somewhere off King's Road and in the quarter saw no reason to do more than slap cosmetics over the grime. When visiting North Soho, however, his other habitat, he was always clean and chic, first bathing in a friend's flat, for he had no running water of his own, and then applying his make-up with impeccable art. We became friends instantly (I'm not denying that the sailor suit may not have been something of a turn-on), and when Simon left for his appointment, Quentin suggested we went to the cinema to see 'One of Miss Hayworth's films'. And so we did, arousing many a curious glance. Later, like Quentin, I too added the bohemian cafés and pubs of Charlotte Street to the diverse worlds available to me on leave, but for the moment I thanked him for taking me to the pictures and took a bus to South Kensington to visit an old school friend of mine called Robin Westgate, a lieutenant in the Guards. We had a nice dinner and I stayed the night in his parents' sparsely furnished London flat, but there was hardly a moment when I wasn't thinking about my meeting with the Surrealists the following Monday.

I was actually meant to be on watch that day, but so adaptable was life aboard the *Argus* that I was able to come to an arrangement with my 'oppo'; he was carrying on with a married lady in Gillingham whose husband worked nights on Tuesday so it suited him very well.

I went up to London around noon and spent some hours in the Victoria and Albert Museum looking at original Lautrec posters in the print room. I forgot who'd told me about the print room but it was open to the public and they brought you whatever you wanted to examine. This fulfilled several functions in my London life at that moment. Firstly it was free so it was a way of staying warm and interested during the day and saving the evenings, as I had done in Wetherby, for drinking and, with luck, debauchery. Secondly, I could examine, in the original, the work of artists who interested me, and linked to that, but rather shamingly, I was aware of the effect of a sailor in bellbottoms asking for comparatively esoteric artifacts, thereby astonishing and pleasing the librarians and the elderly scholars. 'So you're a Tiepolo fan too,' one of them had said on a previous visit. The Lautrecs, however, were not such a good idea. What I hadn't realized was that some of the posters, which I'd known only in postcard reproductions or in the meagre little books of the period, were very large and I had to have the librarian's help in spreading them out, thereby incommoding the gentlemen examining Persian miniatures or Fuseli drawings, forcing them to move, grumbling, into the corners of the room.

When they closed the print room I caught a tube from South Kensington reading, with mounting excitement, one of the Surrealist publications I carried everywhere, and filled in the time in a news theatre and various pubs, in many of which I was stood drinks. Then at eight o'clock precisely, for I had earlier made an expedition to be sure exactly where it was, I entered the restaurant and asked the plump Spanish proprietor where the Surrealists met. 'Mr Mesens,' said the man, 'he go up stairs but no one arrive yet.' To retreat? No, I thought, better go up and drink a glass of wine. I was sure it would be taken as a sign of enthusiasm and commitment. I walked up into a rather dingy room with a large table and sat down at one of the laid places. I was a little drunk from excitement and the beers I'd swallowed. I thought of the pre-war Surrealist 'séances' at the Café de la

Place Blanche in Montmartre. The magisterial Breton, Paul Eluard, Aragon before his traitorous defection to Soviet Communism, Max Ernst, 'the most marvellously haunted mind in Europe', Peret, Miro, Souppault; all those names I had read of, learnt, and in the main mispronounced, from the Herbert Read anthology I had discovered in that Liverpool bookshop.

Mesens, too, with his insistence on the use of his three initials, E. L. T., friend of Magritte, editor of the *London Bulletin*, the magazine in which I had first clapped eyes on a reproduction of *Le Viol, he* would actually be here! I drank three glasses of very sour red wine in quick succession.

There were voices, foreign voices, on the stairs. I forget who came first but I remember everybody who attended that delirious evening: Simon of course, and his sister Sonia, who wore her hair in what would now be called an 'Afro' and had a black boy-friend, Antonio Pedro, a Portuguese painter, two young Turkish poets, Sadi Cherkeshi and Feyyuz Fergar, the writer-cinéaste Jacques Brunius, pipe-smoking, with a long, intelligent, melancholy face and a seductive French accent, and Edith Rimmington, a rather cosy-looking lady whose pictures were nevertheless disturbingly sexual in impact. There were also various girl-friends, all of whom seemed to me extraordinarily glamorous and, I speculated, probably expert in the more erotic games of love and then, finally, E. L. T. Mesens and his wife Sybil, he apologizing in a strong Belgian accent for being late due to the difficulty of finding a taxi in Hampstead. My eyes shone, my spirits soared. I muttered to myself the famous image from Lautréamont: 'As beautiful as the chance meeting of an umbrella and a sewing machine on the dissecting table.'

E. L. T. Mesens, a name which, since Tony and I had first come across it in our pamphlets, seemed to carry an increasingly mysterious weight, was at first sight not especially impressive. Aged then about forty – 'I was born in 1903 without God, without King, AND WITHOUT RIGHTS!' – shortish, plump, neatly if conservatively dressed, meticulously shaved and manicured, his shoes well polished, his hair oiled and brushed back, he had the look of a somewhat petulant baby or of a successful continental music-hall star. His wife Sybil was about five years younger, a handsome, slightly gypsyish woman with an olive skin and fine aquiline features dressed, for that austerely shabby time, with fashionable reticence. Together they presented a certain urbanity far removed (with the exception of Simon, whose style was more suggestive of a country squire visiting London for the day), from the comfortable shabbiness of the other Surrealists. It's true that Edith Rimmington had an expensive fur coat, but she seemed so cosy and provincial, not unlike some of my mother's less dashing Liverpudlian friends, that its effect was negated. Sybil didn't seem cosy at all. She had something of the tension of a beautiful bird of prey, and E.L.T., despite Simon's carefully thrown away introduction, soon established himself as the more formidable figure there. He shook hands with me (this hand I'm shaking has touched that of Breton) and sat down, as if by right, at the head of the table. The boss of the restaurant came up and took our orders, for which we all contributed a pound; there was a law in operation which forbade a restaurateur to charge more than five shillings per head, but by adding whatever the patron thought the client would accept to pay for wine or cover charge, this was easily sabotaged. Feeling like a very minor and impoverished disciple at the Last Supper, I ate my way through a rather underpopulated paella, straining my ears the while to try and catch what Mesens was saying at the other end of the table and chatting to those on either side of me. The girl on my left was Sadi Cherkeshi's mistress. She had short hair and a friendly gamin appeal, but it became clear to me that her principal interest in Surrealism lay behind the Turkish poet's flies. Antonio Pedro proved more willing to listen to my questions and explain who everybody was and what they did, and I was also extremely amused by his vivid Portuguese English. I remember him, that first evening, declining trifle for pudding: 'It is the 'orrible custard and the bread of yesterday,' and also answering my query as to whether the scream of cats in sexual congress on an adjacent Beak Street roof-top was caused by pleasure or pain with 'pleasure for the cat, and pain for the cattess'.

Yet cats and custard apart, I cannot truthfully say I can describe exactly what was said and done that first evening, partly because I was rather drunk and a bit mad with excitement at being there at all, but chiefly because as, over the next few months, I managed to wangle almost every Monday off, I attended most of those evenings at the Barcelona Restaurant, and while certain monumental rows, solemn games, mass ejection by the proprietor, messages from abroad, discussions as to future activities or publications, even expulsions took place, it now seems, almost thirty years later, as though it were one long evening instead of a series taking place in the few months between the Nuremburg Trials, and the dropping of the first atomic bomb.

When I first heard it, the expression a 'Surrealist séance' seemed totally confusing. It suggested table-tapping, trumpets in bird-cages, yards of regurgitated cheese-cloth, and the shrill voices of child guides. I wondered if the intention was to evoke such phantoms as Lop-Lop, Max Ernst's bird-king, or the disturbing spheroid-headed 'personages' of de Chirico. I subsequently discovered that the French meaning of the word was simply 'a meeting', and yet there remained something mysterious about those Mondays. They did indeed reflect a certain spiritual state of mind.

After eating, drinking and general conversation, Mesens would propose a subject. Although he had come to England in 1936 and lived here ever since, he had retained his strong Belgian accent and, despite a wide and vividly-used vocabulary, constructed his sentences as if they were in French. He particularly enjoyed provoking noisy disagreements. One of the more memorable arose out of his suggestion, couched more in the nature of a command, that no member of the group should write or draw for anything except official Surrealist publications. This was all very well for him; his war-work for the Belgian section of the BBC over, he was preparing, with financial backing, to reopen in new premises the gallery he had run before the war; but many of the rest relied on journalism to a greater or lesser extent, Brunius, for example, wrote on the history of the cinema, and even I had begun to review art exhibitions for the *Liverpool Daily Post* at a guinea a time. The opposition to E.L.T.'s near-edict was vociferous and prolonged, and included many threats of resignation and counter-threats of expulsion. In the end, however, the breach was healed.

Most meetings were calmer. I enjoyed especially playing 'Exquisite Corpses', the Surrealist version of 'Heads, Bodies and Tails' combined with Consequences. Opening one of these I discovered someone had written 'Love is fucking' as their contribution. I was astounded. Who could it have been? I looked around at these grown-ups, serious people, some of them the same age as my parents. In the Navy of course the use of the word as an adjective was monotonously obligatory, but here it was used precisely, with deliberation. 'Love is fucking.' I couldn't get over it although I was careful not to betray my astonishment.

After I had served my apprenticeship, Mesens encouraged me to read my poems aloud. These, written aboard the *Argus* during the night watches, offered me an opportunity to dramatize which I was not slow to take up. In one poem there was a line, 'You are advised to take with you an umbrella in case it should rain knives and forks.' One evening I collected a great deal of cutlery from a sideboard and, on reaching the image, hurled them into the air. The effect was very satisfactory, the noise formidable, but while the Surrealists' applause was still resounding in my gratified ears, the proprietor of the Barcelona rushed up the stairs and ejected us all. Mesens was delighted as this gave him, and others, the opportunity to indulge in that other Surreal tradition, 'the gratuitous act', in this case insult. Later in the week the proprietor, not wishing to lose the custom of so large a party on a regular basis, made it up and we were allowed back.

Another near-disaster for which I was responsible took place in the street when we had left the restaurant. I proposed that we should go to a telephone box, choose a number at random and, if and when the subscriber picked up the phone, recite a line from a Surrealist text and then replace the receiver. This was enthusiastically received but when, as the originator of the prank, I was assuring a puzzled gentleman in Ealing that 'The stones are full of guts. Hurrah! Hurrah!' (Jean Arp), a policeman approached and asked to see the identity cards or passports of all present. His confusion was absolute, his desire to translate it into some punitive action apparent. What was a British sailor doing with a group of people of Turkish, Belgian, French and Portuguese origin? However, all our papers were in order and, as I'd hurriedly severed my connection with the crossly perplexed ratepayer in W.5, there was nothing he could do except tell us to move on.

After some months the meetings began to be less well attended. Simon, who, despite the fact that he was the most aggressive in combatting E.L.T., was also the most active member when it came to organization, went away to the Middle East as part of a touring company, entertaining the troops in a production of *Pink String and Sealing Wax*, for he was at that time an actor. Mesens himself was becoming more and more involved in the renaissance of the London Gallery. A lease had been taken on a five-storeyed Georgian building in Brook Street. It was narrow, very pretty if rickety, and in considerable disrepair. The long fight for permits and the frustrating search for building materials were beginning, but the Mesens were soon able to move into the top-floor flat and as by this time I had become very much their protégé, I had another place where I was welcome, another settee where I could sleep.

The meetings became fortnightly, then monthly and eventually ceased altogether, but I didn't really care. I was now 'le petit marin' and, E.L.T. assured me, certain to make my mark on the Surrealist movement. He added that not everybody in the group held this view however. One, whom he refused to name, said that he thought 'I would never be more than the English Cocteau.' I assumed indignation, but was actually rather pleased.

I now had several earths, and, fox-like, chose to keep moving. The Mesens' was certainly the most comfortable and not only was Sybil an excellent and imaginative cook but I was also taken quite often to dine at a restaurant of which I had heard my mother speak of in awed tones, The Ivy. Here I was amazed to find that the bill could be as high as thirty shillings a head without wine, and was equally surprised at the amount of time E.L.T. and Sybil were prepared to invest in deciding what to eat.

Back in their flat I helped hang some of E.L.T.'s remarkable collection (the bulk of it had been stored in the cellars of the Palais des Beaux Arts in Brussels where it had luckily escaped the attention of the occupying and modern-art hating Nazis), and at last was able to examine at close quarters those painters I had admired so passionately. While we worked, washing glass smeared with the dust of six years, spraying and revarnishing canvases from which the images emerged with renewed clarity, he talked to me about the old and heady days in Paris and Brussels: about Ernst's near-murderous jealousy of Miro, of Tangui's drinking habits, of Magritte's meticulously bourgeois life-style. I was enthralled, yet I didn't choose to spend all my time there. For one thing I was worried that I might overstay my welcome. Edouard, even in those days, was a heavy drinker and, in drink, of uncertain temper. For another I was eager for experience both sexual and social, and the Mesens lived, I then thought, rather too ordered and domestic a life to satisfy me. For example I was extremely impressed to discover in his collection Magritte's *Le Viol*, that representation of a woman's body replacing her face, which had struck me as so marvellous when I had come across it reproduced in the *London Bulletin* in the art school library at Stowe, but, when I offered to hang it, Sybil refused. At the time I thought this mere prudery. The idea that she might dislike it on the grounds that it reduced her sex to a purely physical cypher never occurred to me.

London was beginning to acquire a meaning, a pattern. I found myself fleeing to my Liverpudlian womb less often. The kindly elderly Jewish cousins, no doubt to their relief, saw me less often. No so however a connection of my father's family, a girl, some five years older than myself, who was considered the black sheep of the family. Her name was Paulie Rawdon-Smith, the daughter of a rather stuffy Liverpool doctor. Meeting her by chance on my way to the Victoria and Albert print room, I discovered she had a mews flat close by which she rented for a minimal amount and where I was welcome anytime. It was with Paulie that I came to know the pubs and cafés of Soho, re-meeting in this context the immaculately clean Quentin Crisp: 'Mr Melly, I've been led to understand that Miss Rawdon-Smith is your cousin.' Here too I came to know many a famous old bohemian bore like Iron Foot Jack, with his pocketful of yellowing press-cuttings. Jack, dressed in a wide hat, cloak and knotted scarf and smelling like a goat in rut, claimed that his six-inch iron foot was the result of losing part of his leg to a passing shark, an unlikely explanation as he had retained the foot itself. He had a juicy Cockney accent, boasted of occult powers, and lived with a series of old crones whom he used as an excuse for hinting at a Crowleyan sexual virility. 'There are occult practices,' he told me every time we met, 'that it is best the general public know nuffink abaht. When I had my stewdyo in Museum Street . . .'

More interesting was a woman called the Countess Duveen, old and bent, with some indication of a former beauty. She spoke in a grand but rasping voice, kept herself going on the insides of benzedrine inhalers and cadged cups of tea, earning her living from scavenging in dustbins or on bomb sites. She sold me a carved wooden bird of East European peasant origin for sixpence. It had once had a string which, when pulled, made its head jerk up and down to suggest that it was pecking grain, but the string had long since perished and the head sagged permanently forward. 'Isn't it a saucy pussy!' the Countess had cried by way of sales talk. I resisted buying what she described as 'a handsewn gentleman's kid glove' on the grounds that I had two hands. 'I think,' she announced despairingly, 'that I know where I can find the other one.'

Quentin, Iron Foot Jack and the Countess Duveen confined themselves to seedy cafés chosen for how long you could stay there without buying more than the odd cup of tea. In the pubs, especially The Fitzroy and The Wheatsheaf, I met a less derelict collection. The occasional *bona fide* lion I recognized but never dared approach: old Augustus John with his baleful swivelling eye, Dylan Thomas oozing drink and alternatively dozing off or talking frenetically in his parsonical, obscenity-larded posh Welsh bray. Others seemed more accessible: Maclaren Ross with his cloak and silver-topped cane, Nina Hamnet, rushing impulsively from one watering-hole to another for fear of missing out on something. My old schoolmaster, John Davenport, who, depending on how drunk he was, would either hug me warmly or cut me dead, and a variety of queens, anonymous earbenders, young painters, writers and poets, and the more commercially-minded sectors of the armed forces, mostly sailors or guardsmen.

It was a scruffy, warm, belching, argumentative, groping, spewing-up, cadging, toothbrush-in-pocket, warm-beer-gulping world which I found less taxing if also less stimulating than the Surrealist ambience. I slept occasionally with a man who made masks. He had amazing tragic blue eyes, stubble under his make-up and smelt of pungent but not unpleasant sweat. He lived in Frith Street in a tatty but inventive flat with bare boards, shawls, incense, and his own artifacts grimacing in gilded candle-lit rictus anguish: a setting which twenty years later would have seemed a commonplace hippy pad, but at the time was, for me at any rate, completely unique. Here, after the pubs and coffee shops closed, a tough homosexual world gathered to bitch in the accents of Birmingham or Newcastle. As dawn broke we would all collapse in each other's arms on stained mattresses under grimy blankets which had been 'liberated' from hospitals by a skeletal consumptive boy who worked as a porter at the Middlesex.

It was my cousin Paulie who first took me to the Caribbean Club in Denman Street. This place, a lobby bar and a low but large room with a bandstand at one end, was primarily West Indian, with a few black GIs and some white members, mostly girls of rather painful refinement whom in retrospect I imagine to have been tarts. The owner, Rudi, was one of those between-the-war blacks whose English was exaggeratedly Oxbridge, whose clothes were excessively formal, and who once a night would sing, in the rich baritone of Paul Robeson, such sophisti-cated night club ballads as 'East of the Sun and West of the Moon' . . . The rest of the music was more jazz-orientated. A trio led by Dick Katz, smiling like Carroll's Cheshire Cat, played a selection of tunes ranging from Fats Waller to the newly emergent Bebop. Sometimes I would sing a blues, tolerated by the clientèle for my gauche sincerity. The man at the door called me 'Admiral', the barmaid, as long as I had money to drink with, allowed me to flirt with her. I was eventually given an honorary membership. 'Now,' I thought to myself, 'I've really made it. I am a member of a London Club!'

Another bed, or in this case two chairs, I found in Margaretta Street, Chelsea, in the room of the Turkish Surrealist poet, Sadi Cherkeshi. Unlike Simon, who tended to put me off by explaining that 'his mistress' was staying the night and it would therefore be 'inconvenient', Sadi didn't mind me lying in the dark, ears agog, listening to him screwing his girl. I felt no end of a liberated, tolerant and, to be frank, stimulated creature in this role. In the end, however, it was the household which was to prove more central to my life. At its head was an elderly man called Bill Meadmore who wrote biographies, ghosted memoirs and worked for Customs and Excise. Long-haired and irascible, married to a kindly, quietly realistic, humorous woman called Dumps, he was the progenitor of three daughters and the owner of two unreliable cats. Bill and I found ourselves on immediate terms. Not that we agreed about anything. Bill, despite Sadi and, before him, Simon as lodgers, hated Surrealism and indeed modern art in general. He liked Sickert and, in lieu of the means to buy his paintings, had acquired the work of his followers, in particular those of Clifford Hall, a gruff, bearded man with whom I had many a furious argument, stimulated, when there was any danger of it flagging, by Bill's mischievous intervention. It seemed inevitable that one morning, on going to the bathroom, I should come upon Quentin Crisp relaxing in an unpatriotically full tub, Bill Meadmore's being one of those houses where he prepared himself for a sortie up West. Surrealism, Soho, the Caribbean Club, the Meadmores, Quentin, my second cousin – I felt that I had begun to discover, in the seeming chaos of the 'Smoke', a secret village. As spring came however, I was to happen upon a very different world.

Chapter 7

Robin Westgate, the school friend I had been to see on the evening of the day I had first met Simon Watson Taylor, was responsible for introducing me into a milieu far removed from the austere if original morality of the Surrealists or the boozy promiscuity of Soho.

Robin was of a fragile beauty which I had long associated with Wilde's Dorian Gray and was soon to identify with Waugh's Sebastian Flyte. His manner was correct, diffident and charming, but his opinions, even on so simple a matter as the weather, while seemingly delivered with clipped precision, were so qualified as to leave the listener unable to decide whether it was fine or not. His parents lived mainly in a manor house in Essex. His mother was what is called well-connected. His father, a retired major with a moustache, while almost completely silent, somehow managed to project a deeply-grained and melancholic pessimism. I can only remember him addressing one remark to me directly. I had come to see Robin in the Westgate's *pied-à-terre* in South Kensington and found his father sitting alone in a deck chair in the under-furnished drawingroom. I was wearing a cardboard bird's mask I had bought in King's Road and which I believed, in conjunction with my bellbottoms, transformed me fairly convincingly into one of those 'personages' from an Ernst collage. Major Westgate looked at me without showing much reaction but eventually asked me, without any real conviction, if I didn't think that my metamorphosis might be construed as 'an insult to His Majesty's uniform'. Before I could answer Robin came in and Major Westgate relapsed into his customary shell.

Mrs Westgate, on the other hand, was the opposite of inhibited. A great beauty with an unfair amount of charm, she would ask my advice about everything, no matter how intimate; a trait which, applied to someone as young and inexperienced as I was, could not but fail to seduce me utterly. Most of the time, however, Major and Mrs Westgate were in Essex but, as Robin was stationed at Chelsea barracks, he stayed in South Kensington when not on duty and I, from time to time, with him.

At school we had never in fact had an affair, but as everybody thought we had, I had gone to no trouble to put the record straight. To be exact I had cast Robin as Bosie to my Oscar, taking it for granted that this role-playing would be to his liking. Now I would be less sanguine. Robin's ability to fall in with everything or, to phrase it more negatively, his inability to assert himself, makes it difficult to be sure. Yet he had no hesitation in behaving unconventionally providing someone else made the running, even though the consequences might have proved awkward or even disastrous. For example commissioned officers were not allowed to associate with enlisted men, yet Robin never put up any objection to appearing in public wearing his Guards uniform with me in bellbottoms. We took considerable liberties, walking up Piccadilly for example arm in arm whilst eating ice-cream cornets, and on another occasion when

Robin and a platoon of his men were, according to some ancient tradition, guarding the Bank of England overnight, he even went so far as to ask me to dinner there. It was apparently his privilege to invite a guest to help relieve the tedium of this chore, but the Sergeant who escorted me up to the small but formal diningroom, with its regimental silver and excellent wine, made it quite clear that he found an Ordinary Seaman an unacceptably bizarre interpretation of this right.

Much more dangerously he came with me to an Anarchist meeting in the upper room of a public house where I had accepted to speak. The Anarchists, now released from prison, were as idealistic as I had hoped and I was completely bewitched by a woman called Marie Louise Benari, the beautiful daughter of a revolutionary murdered by Mussolini, and the wife (or companion as they preferred to call it) of one of the English comrades. She, and indeed all of them, had an unsentimental goodness and a true vision betrayed alas only by the age-old political and/or religious machinery they hoped to dismantle, and by the willing servitude of the slaves they longed to free. Nevertheless, their philosophy was regarded with great suspicion by the authorities in general and MI5 in particular, and it was completely unacceptable that a member of HM Forces should subscribe to it. This, much later, I was to discover, but at that time, with blind naïvety, it never occurred to me that I was doing anything untoward. Yet dangerous as it was for me to declare my allegiance to Anarchism, Robin's presence, in his smart uniform, was surely far more of a hazard. He sat there, however, as calm as in his mess, listening to my near-tearful histrionics in the name of freedom, and not even flinching when, in what I considered a daring *coup-de-théâtre*, I first played and then smashed a record of the National Anthem I had bought for the purpose in the HMV shop in Oxford Street. Perhaps in Robin's case, it was a profound ennui, possibly inherited from his father, which made him ready to accept whatever anybody proposed. Perhaps it was simply good manners carried to an unprecedented extreme.

Given his parents' empty flat, we finally went to bed together without, I suspect, much enthusiasm on his part although, for a full decade to come, we would occasionally repeat the experience when the circumstances were right. Later he was to take to girls, but like myself, like many public school boys of the period, he was then entirely gay, and his physical beauty was such as to ensure him an immense success, while his good manners prevented him from ever saying no. Meeting him once in the company of the young Lord Montague, also in the Guards, I took them to tea with David Webster. David looked at them with unconcealed admiration. 'I don't know how you do it, dear,' he murmured to me. 'Two of the prettiest things in London.' I glowed with pride.

Robin's main liaison at the time was with an old Italian baron who didn't approve of me at all. I was invited for dinner, but as I preached anarchism and Surrealism non-stop the invitation was not repeated. I was fascinated, however, to see scattered about the rather gloomy, if luxurious, flat a great many signed photographs from the Pope. This fed my fantasies of the sort of Bunuel-like corruption I longed to discover. I breathed in deeply the pot-pourri-scented air and imagined the day of reckoning on the barricades.

Most of Robin's friends, especially as they seemed to like me, produced no such visions of liberating revolt. In truth, chameleon-like, I fell in instantly with their easy-going manner, revealing just enough of my Anarcho-Surrealist leanings to amuse them. It was in such a mood that one fine spring morning, while spending part of a weekend with Robin, we strolled across Hyde Park, along Oxford Street and up Portland Place to meet a friend of his whom he felt sure I would appreciate. It was a sunny morning and the trees in Regent's Park were just beginning to hint at greenness. We turned into a Nash Terrace and rang the bell of a large cream stuccoed house. A butler answered it, seeming in no way surprised to find a Guards' officer and an Ordinary Seaman standing on the doorstep. We walked through a hall and got into a lift. The house, Robin explained, belonged to his friend's parents but he had a top flat in it. We rose five floors and emerged into a rosy-pink world where, standing with a Pimms in his hand, beautifully dressed, discreetly made-up and smelling divine, was a man whose face, before he had said a word, suggested something witty and outrageous. Robin introduced us and told me his name was Reggie Kestrel.

Reggie was then in his early thirties, which seemed to me quite old, but as he took a great deal of trouble with his appearance he looked much younger. He was so obviously gay that the Services were out the question but, as he also suffered from flat feet, the authorities had gratefully rejected him on this ground. Now, relieved from the necessity of doing anything, he was devoting his life to pleasure as far as he could manage on what he claimed was an extremely inadequate allowance from his father. He belonged therefore to that class of person whom the post-war press had already begun to refer to as 'drones'; a category at one time admired or at any rate tolerated, but only minimally less despised than spivs or black-marketeers in the grey dawn of the age of austerity.

His lifestyle, deviation apart, was that of an Edwardian man-about-town. Rising late and bathing long, he eventually sauntered up to the West End to drink hot chocolate in Fortnum's with his circle. He lunched in Soho, usually at Le Jardin des Gourmets where he would flirt heavily with the waitresses (waiters, due to either their nationality or conscription, were a comparatively rare species), in the hope, usually successful, of cajoling out of them an extra, and illegal, slice of gateau generously ladled with cream. Reggie was childishly greedy and was beginning to develop a small but definitive pot, a phenomenon which, as he was also quite vain, caused him a certain amount of impotent anguish. In the afternoons he would go to the cinema, preferably the Curzon, while his evenings were devoted to drink and sex. Superficially this might appear a rather monotonous way of life but he illuminated and transfigured it through his dazzling wit and sense of fantasy, so that even the most trivial encounter became an excuse for high camp anecdotes in the style of Firbank, his favourite author.

Reggie and I started an affair at once. Physically he was in no way my ideal, but his sense of fun and the sybaritic luxury of his surroundings were more than adequate compensation. Brought up to standards of adequate middle-class comfort, I was overwhelmed by his silk sheets, handmade shirts, rich ties, innumerable suits, and especially by his bathroom with its huge bottles of Prince Guerlain, French soap (a present from a thoughtful friend who had helped to liberate Paris), and its vast warm towels. Nor was I unimpressed to discover he was an Honourable. His father, patrolling the house under Reggie's little nest, was a peer of the realm and, despite my knowledge that to a Surrealist and an Anarchist this was not so much irrelevant as deplorable, I found it absurdly glamorous.

I was eventually introduced to his parents, a course Reggie found preferable to bumping into them fairly regularly in the hall or lift. His father looked like a rather dated caricature of an elderly English aristocrat, having a red face and bristling white moustache, and wearing rather old tweeds much patched and mended. His mother was American, a small, animated, prettily bird-like woman who conducted the tea from behind a battery of silver tea-pots, hot-water-pots, milk jugs, cream jugs, sugar-basins, slop basins, tea-strainers and sugar bowls. I was careful to call him 'sir', and they seemed to accept me as Reggie's friend, but I was however puzzled as to how much they knew about his propensities. In this, as in much else, I was naïf.

Often in later life, people have asked me if I have ever been to an orgy or, as the sixties preferred to call it, become involved in 'group sex' and, thinking in terms of heterosexuality, I've always said no, or at any rate only to the extent of a threesome or as a quarter of an interchangeable quartet. In fact at this period of my life I was fairly frequently a participant in mass homosexuality but, thinking of it as simply an extension of schoolboy activities, I never associated it with an orgy, a term I felt to imply a Roman profusion of grapes, wine, buttocks, breasts, marble chaises-longues, and squiffy laurel crowns. At Reggie's, however, there were fairly regular orgies involving Guards officers and other ranks, plus interested civilians, and I found them perfectly acceptable and guilt-free. My speculations about Reggie's parents in no way extended to their butler Grope who not only appeared to think nothing of serving breakfast in bed on mornings when we were alone, but was equally detached in proffering cups of coffee to a writhing mass of bodies or actively horizontal couples strewn around the flat. Despite his rather bland if precious manner, the moonfaced Grope knew his place. He showed no more excitement than if he had been present at a more conventional 'at home' and never attempted to participate. He was, in the true sense, a gentleman's gentleman. As to my doubts as to how much Lord Kestrel was aware of what was going on, these were soon resolved, but the cause of his angry confrontation with his son was not so much to do with what was going on, as the accompanying noise.

I had, of course, tried to interest Reggie in jazz but he didn't really like it, and particularly not as a background to sensual activity. Here he favoured Edmundo Ross played at full volume on a radiogram. There were no LPs then of course but, by stacking-up twelve 78s, he was ensured of about forty minutes' worth of rhumbas, sambas and cha-cha-chas and eventually somebody would turn the lot over. The insistent rhythm plus people falling off beds or over each other, shrieking or giggling, knocking over glasses, and banging away all over the flat was quite enough to wake His Lordship a floor or two below, and though Reggie theoretically asked his guests not to make too much noise, the amount of Pimms' No 1, the drink he usually provided to make things go, ensured that in practice no one took much notice of this request.

On the night in question I had fallen asleep up a very pleasant boy in the RAF. In the ensuing débâcle I found the time to apologize for this breach of sexual manners and he accepted my apologies with good grace – not that there was much time for recrimination even if he had wanted to. His Lordship was standing at the entrance to the flat wearing an ancient fawn dressing-gown with a frayed plaited cord, striped pyjamas and very old leather slippers and shouting at his naked son that everybody must get out at once or he would call the police. Meanwhile, panic-stricken, Reggie's guests were struggling into their uniforms or civvies and hurrying down the stairs. By the time I was dressed –

bellbottoms are quite complicated when it comes to getting them on in a hurry – Lord Kestrel, still in his pyjamas, was standing on the right of his front steps shouting abuse at the departing orgiasts while on his left Reggie, who had by this time put on an expensive silk dressing-gown I had watched him choose in Burlington Arcade, was apologizing profusely for his father's boorishness and asking us all to be sure and telephone him next day. As it was far too late to bother anyone else, I staggered as far as the Union Jack Club, where there was luckily a bed available. I woke next morning at 7 a.m. in time to catch the sailors' all-night-in train back to Chatham, to discover that everyone else in the large dormitory was Chinese, a rather un-nerving experience while suffering from a ferocious hangover. I rang Reggie later; he said his father had calmed down, and I was perfectly at liberty to come and stay with him the following weekend. I did so, taking with me, as a precaution, some flowers for Lady Kestrel. Although as monosyllabic as usual, Lord Kestrel made no reference to the event.

So warm was my reception that I felt emboldened to open my ditty box and get out a copy of *The Liverpolitan*, a small monthly magazine which had accepted two of my articles: one on why I loved Liverpool, the other on a British Council exhibition of Paul Klee which I'd seen on leave a month before. I was very proud of these pieces and suggested I read them both aloud to Lady Kestrel, who was polite enough to listen without yawning and to compliment me at the end. I was even more delighted, however, when on a visit to David Webster a day or two later, I found I'd no need to open my little case. With what in retrospect strikes me as kindly tact, he had placed *The Liverpolitan* on the top of a pile of other publications on a low glass table. 'I've read your little pieces, dear,' he said as he poured me out a drink. 'The Klee piece is a tiny bit naïve but the Why-I-love-Liverpool bit has something.' He picked it up and opened it. 'You do go on about the poetry of the local *patois* rather too much,' he complained, 'but I quite like the rest.' He began to chuckle. ' "When on leave in London",' he read out, ' "I have a very gay time". Now that, dear, I'm inclined to believe, but you really shouldn't let everybody know . . .' I nodded but I didn't really know what he was talking about. I'd never heard the word 'gay' at that time. 'Queer' was in more general use even among homosexuals and indeed above his desk David had hung, firmly between inverted commas, one of those burnt poker-work mottos of the kind displayed behind the bar by facetious publicans. It read 'All the world is queer except for me and thee and even thee's a little queer!'

I actually found David over-critical, as indeed I had while rehearsing Lady Macbeth with him three years before. ('He is willing to listen to any amount of praise,' wrote Pa Watt, the art master, in one of my reports, 'but seems unable to believe that anything less than complimentary could possibly refer to him.') Nevertheless, he placated me by adding that, no doubt, after my demob I would 'take his place in Liverpool'. I was by this time already beginning to think that I must live in London anyway and yet, remembering what a glamorous figure David had seemed to me as a child and adolescent, I could not help but be pleased.

The reason I'd gone to see David on this occasion was actually practical. Covent Garden was to reopen. He had offered my mother two tickets and she had decided to come down and take me. I was thrilled about my mother coming and excited about introducing her to all the friends I'd made and all the places I'd been. I thanked David warmly, and returned to Reggie, who was lying, looking rather put out, in a hot scented bath.

The reason Reggie was put out was that he had discovered he had caught a dose of crabs and, probably correctly, blamed me. I feigned frivolity.

'That'll teach you,' I said, 'to sleep with the Lower Deck.'

I was even so rather humiliated. There was something distinctly unpleasant about finding oneself not only a host to parasites but a transmitter to boot. Immediately he'd told me, I began to itch, and a short search was rewarded. I looked with fascinated repulsion at the almost transparent creature, no bigger than a pinhead, wriggling its legs on the black marble wash basin. I knew about crabs, of course: they were very much part of naval mythology and were referred to by such synonyms as 'fanny rats', 'minge mice', 'mobilized blackheads' and 'mechanized dandruff', but to have heard about them was quite different from catching them. I asked Reggie what you did to get rid of them. He told me rather snappily that he would go to his doctor, but that the best thing I could do was to report to sick bay.

Luckily before taking his advice I confided in Wings. 'If you do that,' he told me, 'they'll shave your bush off, paint you bright fucking blue and confine you on board for a fucking week. There's a chemist in Chatham High Street that'll settle for the buggers.'

I was more than grateful to Wings, as with Covent Garden opening only two days ahead the last thing I wanted was to sit on the *Argus* with no pubic hair and azure balls!

I found the chemist on my way to meet my mother forty-eight hours later. I told him what was the matter and he invited me into his back room which was full of stacked boxes of wartime lavatory paper, Cow and Gate rusks and cartons of Brylcreem. He had a jar of white ointment with him and a little brush. It was clear that he enjoyed this profitable side-line. I dropped my trousers and he made a quick and expert inspection.

'Oh yes, sir,' he said, 'you *have* got 'em!' As he applied the ointment he told me that I was lucky to catch them early. 'I had a Petty Officer in last week,' he said. 'Now e'd neglected them for weeks. They'd got up into 'is chest 'air, 'is armpits *and* 'is beard.' The ointment stung quite badly but then died away to become a rather pleasant glow not unlike that experienced a few minutes after a school beating. It had a chemical smell just verging on the pungent.

'Don't pull your trousers up yet, sir,' he advised. 'Let it work its way into t'roots. That's where they lay their eggs.' He went into the shop to sell a lady some toothpaste and a hairnet. He came back, dived into my bush and pulled out a dead crab, which he showed me, with all the pride of a successful fisherman, on the top of one of the cardboard boxes.

'There you are, sir.' he said. 'Dead as a bloody doornail. You can get dressed again now.'

I did so with some relief. It struck me that he was almost certainly a closet queen, and that part of his interest in the slaughter of crab-lice was that it enabled him to handle the genitalia of the Fleet. As I did up the front flap of my bell-bottoms he said something to confirm this and to make me very glad that I had given him no encouragement to pounce.

'If you don't mind me saying so,' he observed, 'you're very well hung, sir!' Admittedly rather flattered, I ignored this ploy, paid him five shillings and left to catch the train and pick up my mother, who was staying for several days with one of those Jewish cousins of hers whom I had lately chosen to ignore.

The reopening of the Royal Opera House, Covent Garden, was an extraordinarily glamorous affair. Admittedly there was a strong smell of mothballs and the choice of *The Sleeping Beauty* seemed particularly apt as, with clothes rationing still very much in force, most of the women seemed to have recently awoken from a spell of at least six years' duration. Even so jewels, redeemed from bank vaults, sparkled like miniature versions of the great chandeliers above, and famous faces acknowledged each other at every turn. Standing aside at one moment to let a gentleman pass through a doorway I, or more likely my uniform, was rewarded by a dazzling smile from Noël Coward.

After a satisfactory gawp in the bar, along the passages and on the staircases, we took our seats. Programmes rustled. We rose for late-comers who apologized their way along the rows. The musicians infiltrated the orchestra pit and tuned up. The conductor entered and acknowledged his applause, and we stood again for a roll of drums heralding simultaneously the National Anthem and the arrival of the Royal party. Standing ovation for same: the King looking tired and drawn, the Queen smiling as if at intimate friends; acknowledgment of my mother's confession that she felt 'quite chokey'; self-censorship of the fact that I, the Surrealist-Anarchist, felt the same; the dimming of the lights; the clearing of throats and discreet release of waist-coat buttons grown tighter during the duration; heightened excitement at the dramatic effect of the footlights on the great red curtains with their gold cyphers at the corners; the buzz of conversation dying in an instant at the triple click of the conductor's baton and then, at last, with that unique urgency of music heard in a theatre, an experience quite different from any concert hall, the opening chords of Tchaikovsky's overture throbbed out into the rosy darkness of the auditorium.

I quite enjoyed the ballet; it was an enthusiasm of my mother's which, during my adolescence and my total identification with her interests, I had persuaded myself I had shared, although even then I had preferred modern works like *Façade* to the great classical three-actors with their swans and Willis. Now that I was trying to sever, or at any rate stretch, that psychological umbilical cord, I had come to admit to reservations. Besides I had learned from Mesens of Breton's disapproval of the art as a 'bourgeois spectacle' and of how, when Diaghilev had commissioned Ernst and Miro to design the set and costumes for Constant Lambert's *Romeo and Juliet*, the two artists had been temporarily excluded from the movement and the Surrealists had made a noisy protest from the floor. I'd no intention of doing that, but reminded myself to warn my mother not to mention where we'd been to Mesens when I introduced them next day. Meanwhile I tolerated the 'bourgeois spectacle', slightly alarmed by the thought that there might be some parasitic life still active in my pubic hair.

My mother stayed several days in London, her first visit since the war finished, and I was determined to demonstrate my worldliness and *savoir faire*. The meeting with Reggie was a great success. He was exactly the sort of queen she liked, witty and friendly and with a potential title as well, but the meeting with Mesens was far less successful. Edouard took us to The Ivy, by which she was quite impressed because of its theatrical reputation, but, whereas she found Sybil very sympathetic, E.L.T.'s tendency to 'hold the floor non-stop', as she put it, bored her to distraction. She thought him 'heavy going' and 'opinionated', and, knowing little and caring less about Surrealism, she found the evening to be something of a strain.

I took her to the Caribbean as well but she didn't care for

that either, finding it too dark. It was Reggie she approved of. 'So amusing,' she said, and so he was, but my relationship with him was about to end, sexually for ever, socially for a short but bitter time.

In Reggie's sitting-room was a large photograph, taken in the misty Bond Street style of the period, of a very beautiful young man. It was, he told me, his best friend, Perry Edgebaston, who was away in the country. I gathered he was rich as well as beautiful, and I had a feeling that I'd seen him before. Reggie said he'd be back in London soon and of course I'd meet him.

The day of Perry Edgebaston's return Reggie gave a party for him and I asked if I could bring a school friend of mine called Guy Neale who, although entirely heterosexual, even at Stowe, was sophisticated enough to do no more than raise an amused eyebrow if the party developed along the lines that Reggie's parties usually did.

I have mentioned Guy before as it was he who had first played me a jazz record in his study some four years earlier, and who was furthermore the cleverest of that anarchic trio of whom the other members were Tony Harris Reed and myself. I had remet him by chance several weeks before in Sloane Street. Guy, who was wearing the uniform of a corporal in the RAF, told me that he was working in Harvey Nichols, the upper floors of which had been commandeered for the duration, and not yet relinquished. He gave me his office telephone number and we had spent several evenings together. There was something Sphinx-like about Guy. He was tall, rather reserved, and his eyes were of a penetrating pale blue with curiously-shaped pupils, more like a cat than a human being. He said little, but what he did say was original or witty, the words chosen with great care as if they were precious objects and too rare to squander. He painted small, strange, very personal pictures of figures wearing pastel clothes moving purposefully but mysteriously about rather sombre landscapes, and had sold one to Mesens after I'd introduced them. I liked to introduce Guy to everybody, because he was one of those people whose approval I actively solicited, and I would bring him parts of my life as a puppy brings in bones to lay at the feet of its master and looks hopefully up at him wagging its tail.

At school his interest in jazz had led him to learn to play the blues and he had formed a small band with which I was sometimes allowed to sing. It was in this role that he gained the sobriquet of 'Jesus', partially because we felt that jazzmen must always be called something strange like Muggsy or Pee Wee, but mostly because his manner of greeting or leaving his acquaintances involved a smile of beatific benevolence accompanied by the raising of the right hand in benediction. Now in London, we had begun to see quite a lot of each other.

He enjoyed drinking, although only gin, but whereas alcohol worked on me to produce a manic excess, a state he did nothing to discourage, in him it led to no more than a heightening of his verbal fantasies. One night, in a Fitzrovian restaurant, he had pointed out Cyril Connolly, or 'Saint Cyril' as we called him out of respect for his editorship of *Horizon*. Very drunk, I crossed the room and knelt at his feet. 'Thy blessing, St Cyril,' I invoked, 'Grant us they blessing.' Connolly looked rather perplexed to find an Ordinary Seaman carrying on in this bizarre way, but suggested aimiably enough that I write something about naval life and send it to the magazine. I thanked him, rose unsteadily and staggered back to Guy, who had initially suggested the whole absurd enterprise, knowing that, in my condition, I would carry it out immediately. It was he, too, who discovered a talent competition to be held in the Paramount dance-hall in Tottenham Court Road and proposed that, as his piano playing had considerably improved, and I had boasted to him of my success as a singer in naval concerts, we should enter in the hope of winning the ten pounds prize money. We did so under the name of The Melly Brothers but were not even placed. Years later Guy, who enters and leaves my life at irregular intervals, told me how amused he'd been at my insistence on this billing. 'It never occurred to you to call us The Neale Brothers,' he said, 'not for an instant, but then it wouldn't, would it?'

So Guy and I went to Reggie's party for Perry, who arrived

rather late looking more beautiful than any boy I'd ever seen. I *had* met him before. He'd come down to Stowe during my final year with one of those parties of trainee Guards officers who were allowed to spend six months at Oxford or Cambridge to establish their right to return there if and when they came back from the war. I'd come upon Perry sitting on the steps of the Egyptian Entry on the North Front. He was green with drink but even so memorably glamorous. I'd asked him if I could help him and he'd managed a wan smile before turning aside to be sick. Not the most auspicious first meeting but I'd never forgotten him and here he was.

We began to chat and he explained that the reason he'd been out of London was because he'd been to a first night disguised as a Portuguese princess and somehow the *News of The World* had heard about it and were trying to track him down. After a short time we found we were holding hands, a little later kissing, and suddenly I found myself telling him I'd fallen in love with him and he admitted the same to be the case with him. I said we must tell Reggie, so we waited until everybody had gone and there were only Guy, Reggie, Perry and me left and then I told him, and he was very angry indeed.

You might wonder why I found it necessary to tell Reggie at all. He didn't object to casual promiscuity and anyway I could have come up from Chatham without telling him to stay with Perry. I suspect my real reason was largely selfish. I wanted to sleep with Perry right away, but of course I had to rationalize it as the straight thing to do. After all this was love. I needed to commit myself, to avoid anything dishonest or underhand.

Reggie was sitting at his dressing-table when I broke the news. Guy, who'd liked him instantly, was sitting on the bed. Reggie began screeching about treachery, breaking off only to ask Guy, who politely declined, restating his total heterosexuality, to stay the night. Meanwhile, as a physical expression of his anger, he was slapping on rouge and eye shadow and spraying himself with expensive scent. He turned suddenly and drenched Guy with it too, a phenomenon which, as it was very strong, must have taken some explaining away in the RAF office in Harvey Nichols next morning. Perry was a traitor, Reggie told him, and I was an ungrateful little slut. He never wanted to see either of us again. I regretted this but not enough to recant and soon found myself in Perry's service flat in Tite Street and a minute or two later in Perry's huge Jacobean four-poster with its carved cherubs and swathes of fruit.

Next morning I woke to find the curtains being drawn by a white-coated, wizened youth with a very bad complexion and a compliant air. He vanished and returned with breakfast for two on a tray with legs, and most of the newspapers. When he finally disappeared for good, I asked Perry what his attitude was to finding him in bed with a sailor. Perry told me he was quite used to it and not just sailors. Servicemen of all nationalities had left their hats or caps on the hall table, and on one rare occasion when Perry didn't pick up anyone, the waiter had come in with the double breakfast and, with considerable incredulity, had said, 'Alone sir?' before going off to rearrange his tray. Later on we decided to christen this dwarfish figure Fairy Grogblossom after the character in Beachcomber.

I had the day off and so began to get to know Perry a little and to find him more and more enchanting. I was surprised by his flat. The furniture at Reggie's was Harrods 1930s Regency, but Perry's, brought down from his country house in Hampshire, was all real and splendid stuff. To me though it looked rather shabby; the gilt chipped here and there, the original chair covers in need of replacement – the oldest furniture I had till then seen in use, rather than in museums, was Victorian. I was impressed by the flowers however; masses of lilies or orchids in every corner of the room.

Perry and I left it a day or two before making it up with Reggie, but from then on saw him most days we were together. The morning chocolate in Fortnum's, the lunches or dinners at the Jardin des Gourmets were resumed. We all went to the Palladium to see a bill headed by the great Tessie O'Shea wearing a dress of splendidly opulent purple and orange, and alone to Eton for a day of wine and sun which I was quick to equate with the visit to Brideshead paid by Charles Ryder (me) and Sebastian Flyte (Perry), in Waugh's recently published book. I have always had this bad habit of comparing every situation in my life, every landscape or building, with something in literature or painting. It's as if I can only see or experience anything through these grids.

I was really proud to be with someone as beautiful as Perry. I even invited him to tea on the *Argus* and he came, driving down from London in his great Bentley for which, somehow, he always seemed to find petrol. We'd made the mess very pretty with a tablecloth 'borrowed' from the officers and, while my messmates treated this visit with a certain sardonic amusement, they were very nice to Perry and afterwards showed him everything including the engine room, now only used for heating as the *Argus* would never sail again. The old stoker in charge became very skittish as he explained the machinery, obviously revelling in being able to exploit the sexual symbolism so easily to hand. Later this man, a Geordie as it happened, became a perfect pest, showing up when I was alone on night watch and making insistent propositions which I had no intention of accepting. He wrongly believed that this was because I thought his age might have affected his virility. 'When ah git gahin,' he told me, 'Ah'v got a barkboon lak a fookin elephant.'

Perry was very touched by the sailors' ease and friendliness and I was pleased too.

One thing that amazed and rather worried me about Perry was his extravagance. Being an exhibitionist, I thoroughly enjoyed strolling down Piccadilly with him, both of us carrying huge bunches of flowers bought at Harrods, but I was appalled by what they'd cost and I tried to help him mend his ways. 'Perry,' I wrote to my mother, 'was about to spend twenty pounds on a vase, but I stopped him and found him a perfectly adequate one in Chelsea for a pound!' What I didn't realize was that Perry probably didn't find it adequate at all but was too nice to say so. I assumed that everybody shared my middle-class tastes and my belief, if frequently betrayed in the event, in such middle-class virtues as thrift and making do.

How in love was I? I believed totally. I carried Perry's

photograph in my wallet, showing it to sailors in exchange for their thumbed and creased snaps of 'the tart' or 'the wife'; I rang him frequently from the urine-scented public phone-box in the dockyard, and felt a rising sense of excitement as the train from Chatham rattled across the Thames towards Victoria Station, and yet when the break came I felt little more than mild remorse and was able to weep only a few self-pitying tears. Admittedly there was by then something else happening in my life, but I'd expected to feel at least some despair. Not for the first time nor the last did I feel that there was a dimension missing in me. I suspected an emotional frivolity, an inability to scale heights or plunge into chasms. I can cry easily enough but, whatever people say or do, I feel cheerful again in an almost obscenely short time. I have never experienced the gnawing rodent's teeth of jealousy, but have equally missed out on a passion which transforms the landscape. My emotional life, like Coward's Norfolk, has been flat. As to why Perry and I broke up, although it would no doubt have happened anyway, the fault was mine; an example, on a more involved scale, of the 'Melly Brothers' syndrome.

I'd asked him to stay with me in Liverpool and he'd come. It had been perfectly all right, although my mother had found him less 'her cup of tea' than Reggie, but it hadn't occurred to me that Perry wouldn't share my view of this port as the centre of the universe. I took him around to meet my remaining great-aunts, uncles and cousins sitting waiting for death in front of flickering steel grates in Victorian squares or decaying Gothic mansions. I took him on walks through public parks which for me pressed every Proustian button. We drank with my father and his friends in a public house called The Albert, which was for me the exciting proof that I had grown up. I encouraged my mother to tell him stories of her theatrical friends and the parties she gave for them in the Twenties and Thirties. I introduced him to my circle of homosexuals, proud to impress them with so beautiful a friend, and Perry, having very good manners, never let me know that he found any of it less memorable, less extraordinary than I.

Later, after a lot of unsubtle hinting, he asked me to stay the weekend with him in Hampshire. A large Georgian house at the end of a long drive; his mother kind and talkative, his sisters reserved but friendly enough. A butler unpacked for me. An elderly American, a fellow guest, observed how he liked to put out half a cigarette before going to sleep because, relighting it in the morning, it had acquired 'a nice spicey taste'. I was impressed by portraits of earlier Edgebastons, Victorians glowering hairily through discoloured varnish, a Regency romantic with open collar and flowing dishevelled locks, sensible Georgians in front of wooded prospects, melancholy Jacobeans, sly Elizabethans, and furniture that seemed to demand silk ropes across it.

I sucked up to Perry's mother like anything. She responded. Had I a great-uncle who had been an MP? A Sir George Melly? No, he was my great-great-uncle (I suppressed the fact he had no knighthood), a Liberal representing Stoke-on-Trent. That would be he, and she remembered how, when she was very small, Sir George and her grandfather, both very old gentlemen, had walked arm in arm on the terrace after dinner. I glowed with snobbish pride. The Anarchist and the Surrealist never even stirred in their sleep.

On returning to Chatham I wrote a fulsome bread-and-butter letter to her, and a passionate affirmation of love to Perry, who had decided to stay on for a week or so. In the latter I proposed a programme: on my weekends off he and I should spend one in Liverpool, one in London and one in Hampshire with his mother. I took it for granted he would fall in with this scheme. Undoubtedly it helped him make up his mind that it was time for Fairy Grogblossom to serve breakfast to a more varied cast. Next time I saw him he told me an alarming tale, which I believed then but which, in retrospect, may have been a kindly if inventive fiction. I had, it transpired, put the thank-you letter and the love letter in the wrong envelopes. His mother had passed my letter to him along the row of sisters at the breakfast table, announcing rather icily that there seemed to have been some mistake. He had sent my letter to her in the opposite direction. She had not read it and had said no more on the subject, but there was no question of my revisiting the house. I asked him twice more to Liverpool, but he made excuses. In London he became more evasive, and finally, with a certain incredulity, I realized it was over. I asked him point-blank. He didn't deny it. I cried a bit. He was kind but firm. A week or two later I rang up and suggested a drink. He accepted and afterwards, for a time, we met occasionally. I saw less and less of Reggie too. The Surrealist and the Anarchist woke each other up. I began again to visit the Mesens more consistently. I didn't know it but a new chapter in my sentimental education was about to open.

Chapter 8

I had not exactly lost touch with the Surrealists during the Kestrel/Edgebaston episode. It was just that I had seen them less often. Nor had I allowed the world of Harrods and Gunters to destroy my belief in the Surrealist dream or my increasing pleaure in the Surrealist sensibility. Even while eagerly en route to Perry, I had never forgotten, crossing the Thames, to look out of the train window at a building which never failed, or fails, to give me a distinct *frisson*. It is a pumping station, built by some romantic engineer-cum-architect during the last century. It consists of a tall chimney resembling an Italian campanile, but the most extraordinary feature is the pump-house itself. It looks like an imposing French town house with a steep Mansard roof of tiles imitating fish-scales. The house is, at first sight, on two floors with high, regularly disposed windows but, on looking in, you recognize that the façade is only a shell. There are no floors. The entire structure houses elaborate nineteenth-century machinery of great, rather sinister beauty.

In Chatham, too, walking through the dockyard on summer evenings where conspiracies of rusty, geometrical, nautical objects cast their lengthening shadows across the open spaces between railway-like sheds and dry docks, I was possessed by that nostalgic sense of the enigma which permeates the early pictures of de Chirico. I'd acquired my first picture, a little *frottage* of a bird by Ernst. I'd bought it on hire purchase from Roland, Browse and Del Blanco with money I'd earned from writing art reviews for the *Liverpool Daily Post*. Typically Mesens told me I'd been overcharged, but later on was delighted when I persuaded my father to give me forty pounds to buy a *Personnage avec des insects* by the same painter. I took these back to Liverpool on one of the slow night trains, placing them opposite me on the empty seat, staring at them as the train crawled through Rugby and Crewe. Ernst, I thought, Max Ernst, 'the most magnificently haunted brain in Europe', made these things. They are now mine. They have travelled deviously from his studio in Paris during the Thirties to this dimly-lit railway carriage and will soon hang at home. I scrutinized them with hallucinatory intensity. How real was my emotion? I was alone, it's true, but how theatrical were my feelings? I can no longer say. Registering those images, I felt them to be my own passport to the domain of the marvellous. The train rattled over the worn points. The dawn was breaking as I carried them up the platform at Lime Street towards the waiting taxi.

The fact that my father had been persuaded to give money to buy a picture interested E.L.T. considerably. I must eventually learn a trade. Had I thought of becoming an art dealer? Actually I hadn't, but he began to convince me that it was an excellent idea. Admittedly, he pointed out, if I came to him as a trainee I would at first be paid very little, but I would soon advance, and further-more our continuing intimacy would enable me, after gallery hours, to assist him with Surrealist 'interventions' both literary and active. I told him I had thoughts of becoming a journalist but he and Sybil soon shamed me into relinquishing the idea. The press were hyenas, scandalmongers and, to quote Edouard, 'idiots first-class'. I put aside the image I had of myself on the *Liverpool Daily Post*, living at home for next to nothing, proud of my beer-stained mac, nicotined fingers and a sweat-stained trilby worn at a rakish angle. I saw myself now in a gallery, persuading the perceptive rich to collect Ernst and Magritte; my reputation as a poet supported by my guile as a dealer. So persuasive was E.L.T.'s argument that for ten years I 'forgot' that I could write and had been published. Next time I was on leave I spoke to my father about joining the art world and he suggested I ask Edouard and Sybil up to Liverpool to talk it over.

They came, Mesens infuriating my mother by his inability to spend less than three ritualistic hours shaving, bathing and dressing, but my father got on well with him and by the end of the weekend had agreed to buy me into the gallery at the price of nine hundred pounds to invest in pictures after my demob. I was quite surprised by this as, outside the pub, where he was very open-handed, he was rather cautious with money. Nor was he so convinced by modern art as to think of it as an investment. I asked him later what made him decide to do it and he explained that his father had bought him into a business he didn't even like, and at least I was enthusiastic. Later he began to appreciate certain painters, Magritte in particular and after I had acquired *Le Viol* he was always taking me into a pub near his office to see a barmaid who he thought looked 'just like it'. He even began, in imitation of Mesens, to make collages, some of which were both inventive and poetic. 'Tom,' said Edouard, 'is a good old boy.'

I now had a job to look forward to, but as yet there was no prospect of my demob. At some point during the previous year the atom bomb had finished the Japanese war, but I have no clear recollection of when or how I spent VJ night. This is odd because it meant that there was no longer any danger of my being drafted to the Far East to face active service, but I suppose I had become so convinced that I would remain on the *Argus* for ever that I had stopped worrying. When, in a year or so, it was time for my demob, I would drift up to the barracks and remind them I existed, but first there were all those who had been conscripted before me to release into Civvy Street. My life was pleasant enough for me to feel in no hurry, and besides something extraordinary had happened to me, something which entirely dispelled my fast-fading regrets at my rejection by Perry Edgebaston. I had had a woman, and that woman was Sybil Mesens.

One afternoon in their flat, hung now with pictures and furnished with Regency furniture, Edouard and I were discussing sex. As a Surrealist he was naturally in favour of the poetic eroticism inherent in all sexual activity and in its non-rational aspects. The Surrealists had always insisted on the right to act out their desires without reference to traditional moral structures, and with complete contempt for the notion that the only reason for yielding to our instincts was for the procreation of children. I remember asking him, that misty autumn afternoon, why Breton had therefore condemned homosexuality; I had long confessed, rather to Sybil's disapproval, my own propensities. After all, I argued, homosexuality actually precluded the creation of children. Edouard reiterated the undesirable freemasonry of homosexuality in the arts, but told me in fact, among Surrealists, bisexuality was quite common. Eluard, in particular, had enjoyed frequent *partousses* with his wife and other friends. Group visits to the brothel were not unknown, but no one ever confessed to Breton. He, arch advocate of total freedom, the eloquent defender of *l'amour fou*, was, in practice, something of a puritan. It was one thing to write a pamphlet in defence of Charlie Chaplin's fondness for cunnilingus – one of his divorces had raised this issue and the Surrealists had come out strongly on the comedian's side, with a manifesto called 'Hands off Love'; but somehow, when it came down to it, André was overfastidious, albeit defending his position behind the most elaborate and obscurantist smoke-screen. The rest of the Surrealists felt it easier to put his theoretical precepts into practice behind his back.

Sybil was reading a green Penguin detective novel while this conversation was in progress. Edouard resented in her only three things: her singing of Anglican hymns while doing the housework, her fondness for purist abstract art, and her refusal to read anything except what he called 'teckies'; she seemed restless and vaguely irritated with what we were talking about. She shut the book and said quite casually, 'For Christ's sake stop going on about sex. If you want a fuck, George, come in the bedroom.'

I couldn't have been more surprised and looked nervously at Edouard to see how he reacted. He shrugged and said 'Why not?'

I was to realize, long after, that they must have discussed it before and perhaps that part of Sybil's reason was to wean me away from my total commitment to arse. At the time, however, I believed it to be entirely spontaneous. I followed her into the bedroom and we undressed. She was in her later thirties and had a fine body. To my twenty-two-year-old eyes, time had just begun to stake a claim on her; there was a crease under her buttocks and a few lines under her eyes, but she was very handsome, very uninhibited and, rather to my relief, I found I had an immediate erection. I knew, from conversations with my shipmates, what to do: I went down on her and vice versa, kissed and probed and entered. She moaned and moved under me. Looking up at one point I saw that E.L.T. had come into the room. He had taken off all his clothes except for his socks and was displaying signs of obvious excitement. It was evident that he too had enjoyed those session with the Eluards in pre-war Paris·

'You are fucking my wife!' he shouted with fervent satisfaction.

Even then I registered some hidden amusement: that detached sense of the absurd which had always accompanied my pleasure in sex and has made it impossible for me to understand, let alone identify with, the Longfords and Whitehouses of the world. This, however, in no way marred my pleasure and, when Sybil's movements and breathing began to accelerate and her features to change into a mask of rigid lust, I came into her at what proved (but then after all there is not really much difference between hetero- and homosexual climaxes) the right moment.

As I rolled off, Edouard took my place. I watched him with interest and soon felt some restirring of desire. I was particularly impressed by his orgasm, during which he shouted some French blasphemies and rolled his eyes like a frightened bullock cornered in a market place. Indeed for some years I consciously affected this performance until Mick Mulligan persuaded me that it looked absurd rather than convincing.

And so, high above Brook Street, we made love in various combinations and positions while the light faded, and on many other occasions too, but crossing the trans-sexual barrier didn't convert me overnight. I continued for some years to prefer boys and even now, while for a long time inactive in this direction, I find myself staring wistfully at young men from time to time. I had somehow imagined it would be a very different and superior experience, more intense, but it was not. What it did though was to give me the confidence to try again when the next opportunity came; to realize girls liked it too. To make it with a couple proved an ideal introduction. A mixture of the familiar and the unfamiliar proved less traumatic, less of a jump, and I remained ever grateful to Sybil and E.L.T. for their sexual generosity that afternoon thirty years ago.

During the months that followed, now that I'd made it clear I knew it was over, I saw something of Perry, Reggie and Robin. I went to Anarchist meetings from time to time. I went to see *Sweet and Low* and marvelled at Hermione Gingold's ability to make everything sound so rude. I drank, whenever I was up West, in the Caribbean. I trecked to Hampstead to see French films at the Everyman. I met up again with Percy and spent a weekend at his house with his nightmare mother in Aldershot on leave. My fat homosexual friend from Liverpool took me to the opening post-war season at Stratford-on-Avon. We stayed at The Gloriana boarding house. In order to explain why we were sharing a room, he told everyone I was his nephew. I adored the plays, and paid willingly for my pleasure. 'Lovely boy,' he whispered in the Warwickshire night. It was a considerable compensation to be thought this even in the dark.

Mostly, however, I saw the Mesens and in training for my future career followed E.L.T. around as he began to wheel and deal in an art world just beginning to wake up from its wartime hibernation. He had organized an exhibition, 'The Surrealist Eye', at a gallery of a sympathetic dealer who specialized largely in primitive objects. None of the pictures sold; most of them were beautiful. Surrealism was right 'out' in 1946.

'Edouard,' I wrote to my mother, 'took me with him to buy two paintings by Paul Klee (pronounced to rhyme with "hay" not "tea"). They cost him £50 the pair. He took three-quarters of an hour beating down the price from £54 and was very pleased.' I found it rather odd that 'the poet' Mesens should derive such pleasure from haggling over so small a sum and boast about it to me at such length over several gins in a pub off Bond Street.

Later we met Lucien Freud, whom Edouard told me he found to be the only interesting young painter in London, but 'very perverse'. He said that he felt Lucien's main object in life was acting against the theories of his grandfather, the great Sigmund. Lucien, while unshaven and shabby, nevertheless projected considerable *panache*. His guttural Rs advertised his Austrian origin, but his English was otherwise faultless if idiosyncratic. His pale eyes, moving restlessly around the Chinese restaurant where we were dining, seemed more like those of a hawk than a man. They appeared to see through you rather than look at you. Several of his views I found suspect or dotty, but there was no doubting his sincerity as an artist. His passion was to realize, at whatever cost and with ruthless determination, his intense visionary obsessions. Edouard tried hard to solicit his support for the Surrealist canon. Lucien would not be drawn. His amorality, except when it came to his work, rejected totally the idea of any moral imperative.

Eventually E.L.T. went home but Lucien and I sat on. I was much flattered by his interest and unaware that it might have been the product of insomnia. I told him about my perplexity at Edouard's pleasure in beating down the price of the Klees. He didn't find it out of character at all. He told me he thought

Edouard was very unhappy and that his businesslike behaviour was intended to deceive himself and the world. I have sometimes found Lucien's verbal judgments (as opposed to his visual probity), wide of the mark or even totally at fault, but he was right about E.L.T. Inside that extraordinary man a poet fought with a shopkeeper, a drunken anarchist struggled with a man who would check a restaurant bill four times. Mesens influenced me and has obsessed me more than anyone in my life. The surface of my table in the hotel in Berlin where I am writing this at 2.30 a.m. is a homage to his insane sense of order and fantasy, but indeed he was not happy. He needed success like a drug, he rejected success like a monk. His tension drove him to the bottle. He was part saint, part demon, a monster I loved until the day he died of alcoholic poisoning in a Brussels hospital in 1971. In dreams he is my most frequent resurrectionary visitor.

I said goodnight to Lucien and walked towards Victoria Station, where I'd booked in at the Union Jack Club as I was due back on board at 8 a.m. In Regent Street two grotesque old whores were pissing in the gutter. 'Don't look sailor,' they shouted, rather unnecessarily, 'we're 'avin' a piss.'

When I got back to *Argus* I found the ship's cat had done a shit on my hammock. I was not pleased, but, before the end of the day, I was to receive an infinitely more traumatic shock: the Navy had discovered I existed. I was posted to a sea-going ship.

I was on watch on the quarterdeck when I spotted, scurrying along the dockside, a small and agitated Lieutenant with a file in his hand, projecting much of the fussy panic of Alice's White Rabbit. He eventually found his way aboard and after I'd saluted him he asked my name and number.

'Ordinary Seaman A. G. H. Melly, CJX/732558,' I told him.

'Well, where have you been for the last year?' he asked me accusingly.

'Here, sir,' I said.

He rifled through his papers, muttering that they'd had me down as a writer. I explained that I had been indeed a writer but, after failing every exam, had been transferred back into bell-bottoms. He looked as if he'd have very much liked to have put me on a charge if only there'd been one relevant in the King's Regulations. The best he could do was to accuse me, accurately enough, of not bringing myself to the attention of the naval authorities. I remained silent, excusing myself with fake efficiency to examine the credentials of a Petty Officer returning from compassionate leave.

The White Rabbit stood by, impatiently cracking his knuckles. 'Well, now you *have* turned up,' he squeaked crossly, 'you are to report at noon to the main barracks with your kit' (I thought with some dismay of my hammock and its pervasive smell of cat shit) 'with a view to joining, as soon as possible, the ship's company of the cruiser *Dido*, part of the Home Fleet, and currently at anchor at either Portsmouth or Southampton.' (The Lieutenant seemed to specialize in haziness as to detail.)

My 'cushy number' was at an end, but I felt no justification in complaining. It was well over a year since the Petty Officer on duty at the entrance to Chatham Barracks had told me that he'd ''ave me out East before the fuckin' week's out'.

Chapter 9

After a day of medical and dental check-ups, of long waits in offices to have papers stamped and travel warrants issued, after a night in barracks among uniformed strangers, I reported at 0815 hours to be driven down to Chatham station in a naval bus. There was one rating of draft with me bound for the same ship. I was delighted to find out it was Tom Dash, as plump and grubby as ever, with the same mole halfway up his nose. I was delighted because I knew him. We hadn't really got on all that well at Pwllheli towards the end. His refusal to compromise, his working-class chauvinism, his reproachful attempts to dictate whom I saw and what I said and did, made me frequently both angry and guilty. He could be charming, though, and funny, but only when alone. The sound of a middle-class voice, the expression of a middle-class attitude, turned him sullen and boring. He mistrusted my gregariousness, was ever alert for any bourgeois weaknesses.

We held at least the love of both jazz and Anarchism in common, and there we were struggling into the van carrying, not only our hammocks, kit-bags and ditty boxes, but our wind-up gramophones and cases of records as well. I'd almost lost touch with Tom since our training camp days. We'd met once in London and he'd taken me home to his parents' prefab in Dalston but it had not been a success. His father, the dustman, looked at me with silent and gloomy suspicion. One of Tom's posh friends, he'd decided. Tom's cleverness, I suspected, had made him something of an outcast there too. Nor did he want to meet E.L.T. nor even the Anarchists. Now we found plenty to talk about. On the train to Portsmouth we played each other new records we'd bought over the last year. Outside the carriage windows the sky darkened and the trees began to claw the air. We arrived in a storm. There was no bus to meet us so we took a taxi. They weren't expecting us at the dockyard but told us, with that grim satisfaction of those who are the bearers of bad news, that the *Dido* had sailed that morning for Portland.

We tried the barracks, who didn't want us at all, but finally said we could sling our hammocks in one of the offices. As we weren't there officially, they told us, would we kindly fuck off ashore for the evening? We left our things, fought our way in a head wind across the dock road to a dirty little café for greasy pie and chips and then into a squalid and unfriendly little pub next door, where we got very drunk on mild. Staggering back through the howling darkness we missed the entrance to the barracks and found ourselves soaked to the skin and hysterical with laughter, tripping over some railway goods tracks leading down to a jetty and assaulted by angry waves. Somehow we found our way back and, as there was a smelly coke fire still smouldering in the office, were able to dry out our uniforms while we slept.

Next day we awoke with splitting headaches and mouths like Turkish wrestlers' jock-straps to face a freezing blue sky washed clean by the storm, and, returning to the station, spent the day meandering westward along the south coast in a series of ancient and unheated trains. At dusk we arrived at Portland, and there lay the *Dido* at anchor in the Sound. A liberty boat, full of cheerful ratings, tied up at the dockside and we, rather gloomily, took their place and were rowed out to the ship. Stumbling up the gangway to report. I became very much aware that, for the first time since I'd joined the Navy over two years earlier, I was aboard a commissioned vessel.

To begin with it was total confusion, but after a day or two it began to make a little sense. I came to realize that everybody in the ship's company held a different if partial view. For the stokers and engineers, it was the engine-rooms and propellers which signified; for the gunnery officers and ratings, the neatly stacked shells and turrets; for the electricians, the ship was a nervous system of cables and power points; for the writers, a list of names, each entitled to different rates of pay; for the cooks, the galleys and store rooms; for the Master at Arms, rebellious stirrings and acts prejudicial to naval discipline; for the Captain and senior officers a view of the whole, detailed or vague, according to their competence; for the ship's cat, areas of warmth and comfort, and a jungle where the prey squeaked and scurried behind the bulkheads and sacks of provisions. Yet there were also intricate private relationships, both official and unofficial. Every mess had its friends, enemies, and neutrals. Shared duty led to liaisons or enmities. Between ranks, commissioned or otherwise, there were tensions, tolerance, fierce vendettas fought out with the aid of King's Regulations or the sympathetic bending of the rules. There were rogues, poets, morons, conformists, wits, psychopaths, religious maniacs, revolutionaries, buffoons, arse-lickers and good men, all within the outer bulkheads and between the decks. The *Argus* had been no more than a hulk in which we associated out of self-interest and to avoid notice. The *Dido* was a real community, a steel village. At first enormous and confusing, it soon became cosy; not as intimidating as a battleship, not as cramped as a destroyer.

That first night, however, was a mere jumble of impressions and none of them pleasurable. We were shown our lockers, and our mess, ate some disgusting supper where my attempts to make conversation were blocked by the 'I say old boy, what, what,' treatment, told we'd have to rise and shine at 5.30 to scrub the decks, and slung our hammocks, too tired even to unpack. As soon as the tables were cleared I fell asleep, rather apprehensive about what tomorrow might bring. My basic training was so long ago I'd forgotten almost everything. I felt very much the new boy.

I was woken by the tannoy telling me to rise and shine and suggesting we all took our hands off our cocks and transferred them to our socks; a hoary nautical joke which seemed rather less than hilarious at such an hour. On deck it was still pitch dark and there was a medium squall blowing. I was detailed off to sand and canvas the gangway, and then wash it down with cold salt water. While at work on the bottom platform, a large wave soaked me to the skin. I thought regretfully of the *Argus* rusting fuggily in distant Chatham. By the time we'd finished, a few streaks of baleful light offered the minimal in cold comfort along the eastern horizon.

Breakfast made me feel more cheerful, and afterwards I unpacked my kit-bag and stuck up a reproduction of Magritte's *Le Viol* on the back of my locker door. I'd changed my soaking overalls for rather creased number twos, and had a shit and a smoke in the heads, which were doorless and much favoured as a conversation centre, most of the emphasis resting on the erotic adventures of those who had been ashore the night before. Sitting directly opposite me, and regaling the company with such a tale, was a rating I recognized as belonging to my mess. He was large and had the look of an outsize, extremely decadent cherub, but his use of erotic metaphor was far superior to the usual rather tedious norm. 'She was as tight as a mouse's earhole,' he was saying in a flat Midlands accent, 'but so wet that when the cinema organ come up,' and here he splayed out his fingers and looked through them, '. . . I could play stained glass windows.'

After I'd washed and shaved and done my teeth, Tom and I went off to see the Master at Arms to be detailed off for jobs. I had met this man briefly the night before, and thought him as frightening as an ogre. He had a ferocious eye, a snarl and a very black beard. Much to my surprise his office was full of large felt animals: rabbits, teddy bears, and monkeys, which I found inexplicable, but discovered later that he made them for sale and that it was considered judicious insurance to buy one for a child, whether real or fictitious, before going on long leave.

He was very sarcastic, particularly as neither of us had taken any specialized courses, and possessed in consequence no skills beyond basic seamanship. As I was what he called 'posh ignorant', he made me Officer of the Watch's messenger, a cushy enough job with many a chance for skiving while pretending to look for somebody. Tom was put in charge of a cupboard full of mops and squeegees and had to polish a certain amount of brass-work. We left the Master at Arms, 'the buffer' as he is known in naval terminology, with some relief. 'If I had the wings of an angel,'runs a nautical parody of a lachrymose Victorian ballad, 'And the arse of a fucking great crow, I'd fly to the top of the mainmast, And shit on the buffer below.' I felt further acquaintance with the Dido's Master at Arms might well give these words a certain sincerity and I was pleased to escape from both him and his beady-eyed toy animals.

Being Officer of the Watch's messenger didn't excuse me from general duties like swabbing decks, painting ship nor, during gunnery practice, a position in the magazine chamber heaving shells and charges from their racks to the hoists. We put out to sea to do this a day or two after I arrived and very unpleasant it was. Choking from cordite fumes, stomach and arm muscles on fire, the machinery making regular snoring noises like the Red King asleep as it shot the ammunition up to the gun turrets far above, and then the thundering and monotonous vibrations, while enough money to buy a Rembrandt was blown through six barrels.

At 20.15 a shell jammed, and we were ordered to climb to the top of the turret to remove it. To do this we used an instrument like a giant's flush brush. It was pitch dark and the wind howled like forty devils. Nor was the worst over. Crawling down to the mess in expectations of a warm supper and a fuggy unwashed sleep in the grey blankets of my hammock, I discovered that some newly arrived rating with no seatime (it could have been me, but, as it wasn't, my indignation was the equal of anyone else) had been feeling queasy and opened the porthole for a breath of air. With the high sea running, a wave had swept him backwards across the entire mess and by the time those present had got the porthole shut again there was a foot of water to be mopped up. Supper was a cold pie. On the wireless a crooner sang of moonlight and roses. Before crashing I went up on deck to smoke a final cigarette. It was bitterly cold but much calmer. One of the fleet had turned its searchlights on. In its blue beam the seagulls mewed sadly as they wheeled and turned.

Once the gunnery practice was over things became much pleasanter. In a few weeks we were going to sail to Chatham for Christmas, and I was due for a fortnight's leave so that was something to look forward to. Then we were off to the Mediterranean for a goodwill cruise and I was really pleased about that, as I had never been abroad at all. My father had travelled as a young man (he had started his business life in the family shipping firm) but, during my childhood in the 1930s, he was far too broke to consider foreign holidays, even if my mother had been in favour of them, which she was not. She had a terror of the sea, and had only once been out of England and that as a child to the Isle of Man. So it was Wales or the Lake District for us each summer and that was why I was so excited about the cruise.

Meanwhile we sailed rather aimlessly along the south coast, putting into Portsmouth for a couple of days, stopping at Weymouth for no obvious reason. It was a cold stormy winter in 1946. The ship rolled and staggered very badly at times, and I was quite often sick. I particularly loathed that curious feeling of weightlessness followed by the nauseating reassertion of gravity. My mess deck, badly ventilated, was hard to take in the mornings; a mêlée of armpits, hairy calves, meaningless obscenities, farts and coughing fits. My fellow ratings, who the night before had seemed in most cases so charming and in some so attractive, were transformed into red-eyed, green-teethed, pustular horrors. Me too; my feet dirty from the midnight rush to be sick in the heads, I stood in my grey, slept-in underwear and scratched my arse. None of us bothered to wash before our greasy breakfast.

By mid-morning stand easy things had become more bearable. I had already scurried about the ship bearing messages on behalf of the Officers of the Watch, making frequent detours to chat with an increasing circle of friends or acquaintances. On my own mess deck I had come to know the rating whom I'd heard describing his erotic games in the cinema, and a genuine if occasionally frightening original he'd turned out to be. He was called 'the Baron' and came originally from Leicester. His title sprang from his sparing use of the word 'baronial' as an adjective of high praise. Returning on board, he would quite often produce some 'liberated' object from under his mac or greatcoat and offer it for sale.

'Who,' he'd enquire, 'wants to buy this baronial coffee pot?'

On the other hand, anything he disliked, and that included almost everything connected with the Navy, he described as 'Mongolian'. The officers, the Petty Officers, the food, the mess deck, the ship itself, were all decidedly Mongolian. This was predictable, but less so was the catalogue of what the Baron considered to be baronial. 'Big eats', the naval expression for a large meal ashore, usually a steak with an egg on it and a mountain of chips, was to be expected. Grog likewise, and sex, especially in its more bizarre manifestations (it was the Baron who introduced me to the expression 'a yodel in the canyon' to describe the practice of going down on a woman). But in other directions his tastes were more individual. He read a great deal, mostly the English classics, and had a good eye; the baronial coffee pots and other objects he offered for sale were never ugly, and abroad he refused to buy any of the trashy souvenirs which most sailors staggered home with as presents for 'my party' or 'the old lady'. It was however music that especially possessed him, more specifically grand opera and (most baronial of all) Johann Sebastian Bach, a composer he admired so much as to insist on calling him by his full name at all times.

When years later I read *A Clockwork Orange*, the anti-hero, with his passion for 'Ludwig Van', immediately reminded me of the Baron, and when the film came out and people said they couldn't believe that someone so in love with violence, so coldly psychopathic, could also adore classical music, I was able to contradict them, because the Baron was at times very dangerous indeed. Personally I only experienced this once, when some remark I made in the showers offended him, and he threw a bucket of near-boiling water over my feet, but ashore he was constantly and consciously involved in fights. I knew him to carry a knife, and there were times when his face, for all its cherubic innocence, turned very ugly indeed and I was aware that, behind the china blue eyes, a wild beast was insecurely caged.

The Baron was feared on the mess deck. Coming aboard, dangerously drunk, he would pull out his gramophone and play an aria or a prelude and fugue and, even at three in the morning, no one dared to object. Once someone was injudicious enough to suggest, very unaggressively, that he turn it in. The Baron produced his knife and very slowly and carefully sawed through the seaman's hammock rope. There was a crash and a surprised oath as the unfortunate man bounced off the mess table on to the deck, but he knew better than to protest. Putting away his knife, the Baron continued to listen with rapt attention to the divine mathematics of Johann Sebastian.

The boiling water apart, the Baron was in general my champion, although at times this was something of an embarrassment. Almost my first day on the mess deck, I was studying, with a certain defiant ostentation, a new book on Picasso and arousing in consequence considerable scorn among my mess-mates. I quite welcomed this as it gave me a chance to lecture them, to try and make them see why there was nothing absurd in the artist's distortions, but before I could launch into it, the Baron grabbed my principal mocker by the collar.

'Anyone who says a word against fucking Picasso,' he murmured gently, 'gets fucking done over. Have you got that, shirt?'

The shirt in question admitted he had (the Baron called every-body 'shirt' or 'horse' regardless of sex or status). From then on nobody on C deck ever murmured a criticism of the Spanish painter.

Nor was the Baron's protection confined to aboard ship. In a pub in Portsmouth one night I was declaiming and no doubt misquoting Shakespeare when the fat old landlady decided she'd had enough. Looming suddenly over me she told me to get out. The Baron rose from another table and tapped her on the shoulder. She spun round to face his calm yet dangerous regard. 'He can stay, horse,' he told her with mild menace, 'and he can recite baronial Shakespeare,' he continued, 'and if you say another fucking word against it, I'll thump you right between your Mongolian fucking tits.' He sat down again and the old woman retired hurriedly back behind the protection of the bar.

Yet despite or indeed because of the Baron's determination to protect me against slight or insult, I usually avoided going ashore with him. This didn't actually offend him. A night without a brawl seemed to him incomplete, but he knew I in no way shared this view and, if I had been dragged in by accident, I might well have got seriously hurt. Nor was I any help in his sexual forays, as, with my rather obvious effeminacy, I could easily give the rather tough women he favoured the wrong impression as to his own inclinations; for, despite complete sexual tolerance, the Baron was entirely heterosexual. If we met ashore by chance, and he was not yet too drunk, we'd greet each other affectionately. If I realized he was far gone I would do my best to avoid him. Any contact with the Baron was potentially dangerous, but his originality, his wit, his edge, made it a price, within limits, I was prepared to accept.

'You realize, of course, that if what you claim to have done was true, and what you assert you would like to do was meant, it would be impossible for us to remain friends or even acquaint-ances.'

The speaker was an enormous young man over six feet tall.

He had a nose like the Duke of Wellington, a deep voice betrayed when amused by a surprisingly high-pitched giggle, and that serious and civilized approach to life, marred only by a certain pomposity, which is characteristic of those educated at Winchester. His name was Gerald Aylmer, his nickname 'Felix' after the celebrated actor of the time, Felix Aylmer, and this prefect-like explosion was provoked by overhearing in the showers a discussion between an elderly Leading Seaman and myself as to the physical beauty of a boy-rating who had just joined the ship and whose skin, as the killick put it, was 'as smooth as a tombola ticket or a wardroom plate'.

I told Felix that what I said I'd done was true, and what I said I'd like to do was equally accurate if, alas, not necessarily feasible, and that he was not a ship's prefect or responsible for house spirit on board the *Dido*. Suddenly he laughed and agreed that my sexual tastes were indeed no concern of his, and would I like to go ashore with him that night? So we did, and got roaring drunk and became the best of friends.

Felix was a remarkable man. His father was a retired admiral living, as I was to discover, in a village near Weymouth and, as Felix was extremely clever, he could certainly have obtained a commission. I was sometimes puzzled as to why he should have chosen to remain a rating (he was in charge of the ship's charts) but eventually came to the conclusion it was because he was a convinced Socialist. There was a kind of dogged nobility about him, an admirable probity which made me feel flimsy and frivolous, but in fact, once he had recognized and rejected the sixth-form prudery which had sparked off his outburst in the washroom, he revealed a love of gossip, a delight in alcoholic excess, and a shared enthusiasm for many modern authors, in particular W. H. Auden, which quickly reassured me.

The chart-room was high up in the ship, conveniently near the bridge, and Felix, when we were in harbour, was allowed to sleep in it and use it as a kind of study. As our friendship ripened I was invited frequently to visit him there, sometimes with Tom or other friends, sometimes alone. It proved a blessed retreat from the hurly-burly of the mess deck.

Felix was committed to the recently elected Labour Government, and would argue with me frequently as to the need for reformist and gradual political re-education, for the virtues of austerity and control, of the undoubtedly boring but entirely necessary work of committees and sub-committees engaged in such work as the implementation of Lord Beveridge's recommendations for a National Health Service. He viewed my Anarcho-Surrealism as an amusing aberration. He had read History and drawn his conclusions. Nevertheless, he was not uncritical of the Government when he felt them to be at fault and one morning, delivering a message to the chart-room, I found him, the colour of a turkey cock, growling over a copy of the *Daily Mirror*, a paper he had hitherto championed for helping persuade the electorate to reject Churchill. The reason for his anger was an article supporting Ernie Bevin's blockading of Palestine and the harassment of the Jewish refugees. This appalled Felix on grounds of both reason and sentiment. I told him that actually I knew little of the rights or wrongs of the question, feeling only that, after the horrors of the death camps, my mother's race was surely entitled to every consideration.

That evening Felix, the prototype WASP, lectured Tom and myself on the history of Zionism, and in particular on our moral need to honour the Balfour Agreement whatever the political inconvenience in doing so. He spoke well and eloquently (he was later to become a history don), and the upshot was that we all three solemnly undertook to refuse orders, if sent to the Mediterranean, to prevent refugees from reaching their promised land, and, more immediately, to write a letter of protest to the *Daily Mirror*. Our first undertaking was luckily never to be put to the test although I hope and believe we would all three have honoured it. The letter, however, was both written and dispatched. Servicemen were not of course allowed to communicate with the press, but we asked the editor to inform his readers that we had supplied him with our names and ship. This was an unnecessary precaution as the letter itself, written mostly by Felix, closely argued and of great length, remained inevitably unpublished. It might have appeared in print in *The Times*,

Guardian or *Telegraph*, but there was no possibility that the popularist *Daily Mirror* could have seen its way to use up its still-rationed space on so weighty a reproach. Felix, however, felt the better for writing it.

Tom and Felix got on moderately well. Both were keen on chess and would play together up in the chart-room whilst I, whose mind has always found it difficult to remember the moves, let alone plan strategy, read or wrote. They were never close however. Something abrasive in Tom, probably his resistance to the middle classes, forced him to try Felix's patience whenever things seemed smooth or pleasant. My patience too. There were times I hated Tom. Nevertheless it was with him I went down into the cable-locker flat to play our records. For one thing, Felix was not very interested in jazz, and here at least Tom and I could forget our differences, and sit listening to Jelly Roll, Louis, King Oliver, Bessie, Muggsy, Sidney Bechet on the wind-up gramophone among the great coils of the anchor chains.

'I ain't here to try and save your soul,' moaned Bessie in ecstatic glee, 'I'm only here to try and save your good jelly roll.'

The difference between proletarian Dalston and middle-class Liverpool was temporarily erased. The joyful hedonism of the stomps and marches, the catharsis of the blues were all that mattered.

Yet whereas my theoretical admiration for the working class was frequently and provokingly stretched to breaking point by Tom, my third great friend on the *Dido* sprang from exactly that area which I somehow felt it was all right to despise – the *petit bourgeoisie*. Edward Wood came from Arnos Grove. His parents lived in a semi and his father worked in a bank. He too had done so before being called up and was to return after his demob, but he blew every theory I held about the sterility of the lower middle classes sky high, or at least he would have done had I found it possible at that age to compare my theoretical stances with my feelings and experience. Edward was funny, mildly subversive, freshly good-looking, completely hetero-sexual and almost unfairly charming. It's difficult to describe

Edward's golden charm. It was just that he emanated what the hippies, still at the time in their wombs or prams, were to call 'good vibes'.

These then were my friends, with the Baron as a kind of unreliable third option and the ship's writer, a Bambi-eyed South London gay as a confidant and sometimes lover when I really needed to let my hair down. There were others I was fond of, particularly a Welshman called, without, I'll agree, any startling originality, Taff, but as Taff was a constant deserter and in consequence either in the ship's cell waiting to be court-martialled, or else doing time in the glass-house, our friendship had little time to mature.

My relationship with the Petty Officers and Chief Petty Officers was, as usual, cordial, if flirtatious. When in harbour, for they would in no way trust me to steer the ship, I became temporary Quartermaster, a watchkeeper's job involving little more than making announcements through the tannoy ('I wish you wouldn't say "wakey, wakey" so fuckin' womanish,' complained one grizzled Petty Officer. 'It's fuckin' embarrassin' getting up wiv an 'ard on'). As for the officers I found them quite difficult to deal with because they were structured to think of ratings as working class, and swung between a somewhat awkward and patronizing acknowledgment that I was not when they were drunk, and a prefect-like severity when faced by my failings as a seaman.

The Captain was a harmless, rather short man with whom I had little contact, but the Commander, a tall, introspective figure took, for reasons I have never been able to fathom, a paternal interest in me, and did all he could to make my life agreeable. He was also responsible, on several occasions, for rescuing me when I could have found myself in some trouble. Both times my peril was due to the machinations of my one serious and implacable enemy on the *Dido* – inevitably, it would seem in my case, a Warrant Officer.

My first contact with this man was when I had been detailed off to mop up a quantity of water that had been spilt on the quarter-deck. On my knees, dreaming of something else, I became aware of a pair of highly polished shoes standing nearby. Looking up I saw a thin, bitter-faced man regarding my activities with sardonic interest. 'You have never watched your mother mopping up your kitchen floor, have you?' he said mildly. I admitted I hadn't. 'She had a maid to do that I dare say,' he suggested. I agreed she had. He asked me if I'd been to a public school. I admitted it. 'I thought so,' he said and then explained that he had reached these conclusions by watching the way I was mopping up the water into the cloth only to squeeze it out again, well clear of the bucket. I looked down again to make sure he was right and had to agree it was so. I smiled up in what I hoped was an ingratiating manner but this seemed to trigger off a great deal of controlled anger. A nerve pulsed in his left temple as he ordered me icily to my feet. I got up. 'At attention,' he snapped, 'and give me your name and number.' I did so. 'I'll be watching you, Ordinary Seaman Melly,' he snarled, 'I'll be watching you from now on. Now mop up that water,' and he strode away.

From then on he kept his promise, and for my part I accepted the war and enjoyed it. For example I developed a slight eye infection and the Medical Officer said I should wear dark glasses on deck. I went ashore and bought a pair with extravagant up-swept pale pink rims. Most of the officers and the crew found these an excuse for humour at my expense (something I've never minded), or simply comic in themselves. Not so Warrant Officer Perkins. He stopped me and told me to take them off. I refused and produced the Medical Officer's chit. He ordered me to replace them. I questioned his right to specify the kind of dark glasses I should wear especially, I added, as the Commander had told me he found them 'endearingly absurd'. Perkins turned on his heel. He could afford to wait his chance.

The rest of the ship's company have faded from my mind. I remember the leading seaman in charge of our mess, one or two faces remarkable for their beauty or ugliness, the Chaplain, a Welshman given to freewheeling *hwyl* in his short sermons in the recreation space but enthusiastic about the arts and, as was to be proven, distinctly liberal in his attitudes. There was one rating, however, whom I remember clearly. He was the Earl of Dudley's son and referred to, by most of the Petty Officers, as the ''orrible Peter Ward'.

Peter Ward had been evacuated at the beginning of the war to Canada and had acquired a slight Canadian intonation. He had not acquired any democratic principles though and as a conscripted rating on a cruiser, found himself surrounded by those who exorcised their unease at his title and arrogance by continuous mockery. This seemed to roll off Peter's back. What he found far more distressing was having to behave as an inferior to the officers while they, in their turn, sensing his ill-suppressed contempt, went out of their way to see he jumped to it. Looking around for a friend he chose Felix, who had gone to Winchester and, in that his father had been an admiral, was by definition upper-middle class. Being friendly with Felix he was forced, at times, to be at least fairly friendly towards me, but my lack of form distressed him, my political views and belief in sexual freedom appalled him, and my friendship with Tom or the Baron made me unacceptable when in any company except Felix's. Even here though one of the stronger links between Felix and myself, our literary interests, drove him into a sullen rage as above all else Peter was a most committed philistine.

It was with this cast of characters that we cruised up and down the south coast during the winter months.

Edward, Felix and I had begun to draw our rum ration and, before going ashore, we would all give three tots to one of us in rotation, believing that the resultant intoxication would produce a feeling of uninhibited fantasy that would take us all into absurd adventures. This it frequently did. One night in Weymouth we staggered from The Boot, a public house preferred by the Baron to the even more baronial Belvedere, aware, with some relief, that he himself would be in neither as he had been sent to his native Leicester to give evidence at the trial of a mate accused, no doubt with every justification, of stealing a car ('the judge was a right mongolian cunt,' explained the Baron on his return). In the Belvedere was a collection of very mangy old whores and we sat drinking brandy, and listening with delight to their Rabelaisian banter. One toothless Irish lady, with stringy hair cut like a man and pyjamas worn under her trousers, was asked by a drunken Yorkshire Petty Officer how much she'd charge for 'all night in'.

'All night in what?' she asked him. 'We got rabbits in the bloody air-raid shelter!'

'But lass,' he persisted, 'I've got eighteen inches.'

'Uncontrollable passion eh? Well wrap it round your neck and throw snow balls.'

A few weeks before Christmas we met up with the entire Home Fleet for a rehearsal of an event which was to take place in February. The King and Queen were to visit Canada and we were to cheer them off. We were lined up and told that after the salute (to be represented on this occasion by five instead of twenty-one guns), the bugler would sound off a 'G'. We would then raise our caps at an angle of forty-five degrees, holding them by the brims, the arms fully extended, and, when the officer on the bridge shouted 'Hip, Hip', we would yell 'Hurrah' three times, replace our caps and stand to attention. A small sloop representing the *Vanguard* passed between the two lines of ships, and we raised three feeble cheers. 'Not bad,' said the Commander through the loudspeakers, but then he was always agreeable to everyone.

My anarchic sentiments thoroughly stirred by this chilly exercise, I went down to the mess deck and scribbled the beginning of a letter to my mother: '. . . for whose benefit? The King's? Ours? The sentimental heart of the great British public stuffed with *Daily Mirrors*? No wonder constitutional monarchy, particularly the English brand, so appeals to Salvador Dali!'

Then I went up to the recreation space to play tombola, the bingo of the Navy, with the Baron, who always insisted on calling it 'Thomas Bowler'. I won ten shillings. After supper I picked up an American comic. Adding to my mother's letter I commented: 'featuring supermen and desperate criminals who discover how to destroy the world. These bright gaudy pages crammed with sadism, near-rape and death are a wonderful psychological mirror. There is even a Surrealist interest, e.g: "Like evil things spawned by the brooding marsh".' Now if only I'd pursued that line, taken it as the subject for the article nervously solicited by St Cyril in the restaurant, I might have earned my place as the first prophet of English pop art, but I didn't. I slung my hammock and the next day we upped anchor and sailed for Chatham and the Christmas leave.

Christmas was as it had always been. Lunch at my maternal grandmother's, where my father complained, as usual, that Uncle Alan's cocktails had too much orange in them and not enough gin. Even so there seemed to have been quite enough gin for my grandmother, who made a speech, after the pudding and mince pies, in somewhat incoherent praise of the police, sentiments hardly likely to appeal to my anarchist sympathies.

A more expected assault on my convictions came when Uncle Alan himself, always a convinced patriot, insisted on everybody listening to the King's speech to the soon-to-be-dissolved Empire, and then on us all standing, he inadvertently wearing his pink paper hat from a cracker, for the National Anthem. I had threatened my mother to remain seated that year but, in the event, compromised by pretending that the unaccustomed richness of the lunch necessitated a diplomatic visit to the lavatory.

Leave over, I returned to the *Dido*, looking forward to the spring cruise in the Mediterranean, and with a watchkeeper's job which would allow me over the next few weeks to renew the pleasures of the capital.

The London Gallery was beginning to take shape. Edouard had been to Belgium and returned depressed by Surrealism there; 'Very provincial,' he grumbled, and he was furious too that Magritte, in the after-glow of wartime resistance, had joined, for what proved to be a very brief period of time, 'the Stalinists'.

Reggie and Perry were much as before, although Perry told me he was thinking of taking a job, an idea I actually found quite shocking. I revisited Soho, and the Caribbean Club, but now that I was to come and work in London, I found myself beginning to view the city in a new light. I had begun to think of myself as a native.

Halfway through January disaster struck. The ferocious black-bearded Master at Arms sent for Tom and me and told us in his office, largely denuded of toy animals by the Christmas rush, that two ratings of the battleship the *Duke of York* were being loaned to the *Dido* for two months to do a gunnery course, and that two ratings from the *Dido* must be handed over in exchange.

'I know you're mates,' he said, 'and I also know that, with the exception of the 'orrible Peter Ward, you are the most useless pair of fuckin' articles on the ship, so you it is. In repayment of my kindness in sending you off together I shall expect from you, Ordinary Seaman Melly, two free tickets for the Chelsea Arts Ball where I am led to believe a great deal of shagging is the order of the day. You will join the *Duke of York* next Thursday when we reach Weymouth. Any questions? No? Then piss off!'

We thanked him and did as he advised, but I had mixed feelings about two months alone with Tom. I was also upset not to have Felix and Edward to go ashore with as, despite the fact the whole of the Home Fleet were cruising in the Mediterranean, the ships were not necessarily going to the same ports. However, there was nothing to be done, and the following Thursday morning found us sitting in a cutter, one of whose crew was indeed 'the 'orrible Peter Ward' himself, covering the three hundred yards that separated the two ships. There was a gale-force wind, and it took over twenty minutes to reach the *Duke of York*. We climbed the enormous gangway to discover a fo'c'sle like a limitless plain. I was immediately frightfully homesick for the dear little *Dido*, which I had once found so alarmingly large, and I especially hated that instant loss of identity which is the effect of joining any new institution whether a ship or a school. The next day we got up at 6 a.m. to sweep the deck prior to saluting the King. It was very cold and I got my feet wet. Tom and I, sitting down to breakfast without washing, a normal practice on the *Dido*, were shamingly ordered to go and do so by the mess killick, a Leading Seaman.

At 11 a.m. we fell in. The two lines of the Home Fleet

stretched as far as I could see, battleships, cruisers and destroyers fading into the distance. They fired the full twenty-one guns this time, and between the heads of two stokers who were pretending to commit sodomy I caught a glimpse of the King as he passed by a hundred yards off, standing on the deck of the *Vanguard* and saluting his acknowledgment of our rehearsed cheers. One of the stokers had a huge and angry boil on the back of his neck.

The next day we sailed for the first postwar Home Fleet goodwill cruise of the Mediterranean. I had the first watch on the bridge that night: black sea, white spray, brilliant stars. The following morning, in the Bay of Biscay, we ran into what a Chief Petty Officer assured me was 'the worst bastard storm', he'd ever encountered in thirty years of service. Apart from our watches we were forced to stay down below for four days and nights. In consequence there was nothing but the slow sickening roll from side to side, the vile taste in the mouth, the repetitive mess deck obscenities, uneaten meals congealing in fat, spew in the heads and flats, pale-faced creatures barging into each other like zombies, and the throbbing of the machinery. Nobody washed or shaved. Only during my watches on the bridge, stirred by the raging seas, could I feel any exhilaration or purpose in living. I was sad when my four hours were up and I had to go back into the foetid hell below decks.

Then one morning we woke to find the sky a warm bright blue, the waters calmed and sparkling, to port the mountainous coast of Spain. Happiness flowed through the great ship. We cleaned up the flats, heads and messes, shaved and showered, whistled and hummed. My job that day was to paint those strange naval objects: ringbolts, bollards, fairleads and shackles, which sprouted from the wooden deck of the fo'c'sle. Gulls wheeled and circled overhead as white as washing, and for the first time, with ecstatic disbelieving pleasure, I watched the grinning dolphins romping and plunging in our wake.

Chapter 10

Gibraltar is a very British piece of abroad with its Boots and W. H. Smiths, but for Tom Dash and me it was as foreign as could be. At about 3.30 p.m. on the next afternoon we fell in, eyes shining, to enter harbour. The guns fired a noisy salute and by 4 p.m. the great ship was secured alongside the jetty while, in midstream, the *Dido* was moored to a buoy. We both wished we were back aboard her, but at least, that night we could go ashore.

Next to us was an American battleship with several variants on our own more traditional tannoy announcements to laugh at. 'Liberty guys to glamourize' was one such.

We fell on deck at 6 p.m., but before we were allowed to march ashore the RPO read us a bizarre warning from the Admiral commanding the Home Fleet:

'There have been of late several incidents in Gibraltar to the discredit of the service. It is up to every man proceeding on shore to behave in an exemplary manner, not only to redeem the Fleet's good name, but also for their own sake.

Actions in Gibraltar are liable to be misinterpteted so the wise man proceeds with circumspection. Alcohol in Gibraltar is liable to be of an explosive nature, so the wise man is moderate in his intake. The local 'jungle juice' and 'merry-merry' should be avoided. Most of the public houses are in or near Main Street, where public lavatories are few and far between, so the wise man asks for and uses one on the premises before leaving. Urinating –

'that means pissing,' interposed the RPO helpfully

– in the streets is a very serious offence. Commanding Officers are to see that all Libertymen understand these instructions, which are to be read aloud and explained.'

After listening, with ill-concealed hilarity, to this little catechism and delighting in its balanced mixture of officialese and almost Biblical reiteration, we were allowed to go.

We marched through the dockyard. The sunset looked like the disembowelling of a tropical bird. The twilight was both violent and sensual; houses and colonnades swarmed with unseen watchers. Cacti and palms embodied our excitement; even the advertisements for Nestle's Milk, being in Spanish, read like poetry. In Main Street fat shopkeepers stood at their doorways selling rubbish, but we did find some Edwardian postcards. In one of them a man with a long moustache sat dreaming on a balcony. In the smoke from his cigarette, a young woman, whose dress was covered in tinsel, had materialized.

We went into a café called the Trocadero and ordered Vermouths from a Spanish waiter with beautiful eyes but a skin badly disfigured by smallpox. On the stage a fat woman in red and gold net danced for the Fleet. I bought a cake made of cream in the form of a rose. It had no taste. We smoked cigars and moved from bar to bar. We came across one of our Petty Officers

alternately embracing a blonde whore and eating cheese sandwiches. On the other side of the room four sailors were beating
up a fifth, but were so drunk as to make little progress. Nevertheless, the boy wept bitterly, his hair hanging over his eyes.
Various other matelots were dancing together. Others, ignoring
the notice 'No men allowed on the stage' were singing 'Maggie
May'. Tables were overturned, glasses broken, and the manager,
sighing resignedly, charged more and more for his raw alcohol
and blackcurrant juice.

'Not only to redeem the Fleet's good name, but also for their
own sake . . .'

As we reeled back to the ship, singing 'Nobody knows you
when you're down and out' and reciting bits from Stephen
Spender's translation of Frederico Garcia Lorca, we could not
but fail to observe that, on every corner, unwise men were
relieving themselves with evident satisfaction.

Next day Tom and I spent the morning on some low rocks from
which the British Fleet emptied its gash (rubbish) into that
tideless sewer, the Mediterranean. Our job was to burn out
paint pots, a very satisfactory occupation, yielding a pleasure not
unlike picking one's nose. As we worked, some of the Spanish
dockyard maties, admitted daily into Gibraltar to earn their
living, turned over the mounds of rubbish in a search for half-
eaten sausages or scraps of meat, which they dried on a wooden
box and then ate with relish.

Despite the fact that the workmen were on British territory,
Tom and I saw this as a symbol of Franco's exploitation of the
working class. Spain, being so close and, with the exception of
Portugal, the sole remaining bastion of Fascism in Europe, had
an almost pornographic effect on us; that is to use the word
'pornographic' in the sense of arousing simultaneously both
excitement and revulsion. Spain, we felt, had been the 'pure'
war. While secretly disagreeing with the British Anarchists in
feeling that the struggle against Hitler was simply one corrupt
force opposing another, we still thought of Spain as the great lost
cause. There, before it had been crushed by the Stalinists,

Anarchism had been a reality and not simply an ideal, had inspired action and fired guns. The death of the Republic had been mourned by a galaxy of talent: Auden and Isherwood, Spender and Connolly, Picasso and Miro. Like many of our generation we were infatuated with Lorca, a poet now seldom mentioned, and whom we believed (for later on the authors of his death were to become much dispirited), to have been shot by the Falangists. In retrospect, the Civil War has come to seem more like a vivisection laboratory where two equally cynical and authoritarian powers experimented, under ideal 'field' conditions, with the techniques of sophisticated destruction. Some had already recognized this, but the message had not yet got through to us. Spain was more a state of mind than a place. Among the burning paint pots and scavenging dockyard maties we looked across the Straits to Algeciras and dreamt of freedom.

We couldn't go ashore that evening but there was some very interesting news. On our return from Villefranche, our next port of call, there was to be an expedition to Seville via Jerez on offer to all members of the Fleet, both officers and men, at six pounds per head. Apart from the six pounds there was another condition: we had to wear civilian clothes – no problem for the officers, who went ashore in them anyway, but an obstacle to us. Not an insurmountable one, however. Tom and I immediately put our names down and wrote home; both of us for our civvies and me for money as well.

Next day was a 'make and mend' so, although we were meeting Felix that evening, Tom and I decided to go ashore early and walk up the rock to see the apes. Alone, released from social and class pressures, we were truly happy and at peace. We climbed in brilliant sunshine and showers of rain, through woods smelling of leaf mould and fern, past villas where children in red dresses played with hoops and white doves sat in the branches of olive trees. Cacti threw fantastic shadows across our path. We saw a child's swing hanging in a grove. High up, from the north face of the rock, we could see the bull-ring of Lalinea.

'Oh black bull of sorrow! Oh white wall of Spain!' we quoted simultaneously. We picked narcissi and stuck them in our hats.

At last we found the apes, the responsibility of the Army, guarded by two friendly Tommies almost as agile as their charges. There were four large males in the enclosure, eight smaller and more active females and several babies, like kittens with the faces of sad old men. One of the males sat on an iron bar with a three-hundred-foot drop beneath him and made water. We'd a quote ready for that too, although not from Lorca: ' "All is not gold that glistens," said the monkey, "as he pissed in the sun." '

Towards evening we came down into the town and met Felix, who had the 'orrible Peter Ward with him and we got very drunk. Felix's deep booming voice and magnificent laugh put us all in the best of humours, and the evening turned into a kaleidoscope of full and empty glasses, eyes, paper flowers, breasts, cigars, castanets, nuts, oranges and darkness. The Liberty guys, suitably glamourized, were everywhere but there was no inter-fleet fighting. At one point Tom and one of the American sailors changed hats. We met the Baron, who bought a round of drinks to toast 'all Weymouth whores'. A Yank staggered up to Felix and asked him if he gave head. Felix said he didn't.

'Goddam it,' said the Yank. 'You've lost me two mother-fucking dollars.'

Quite suddenly, with that illusory and inexplicable speed which is a side-effect of drunkenness, Felix and Peter vanished, and Tom and I found ourselves trying to persuade a rather solemn Negro US army officer that the basis of society was criminal.

'I've been in the Pacific,' he told us somewhat irrelevantly, 'but I believe, yes sir, I believe in the good book, the Bible.'

It was pouring with rain and we took a taxi back to the *Duke*. Next day we heard that Felix had been arrested trying to crawl across the Spanish border. Pissed as a newt and covered in mud, he had spent the night roaring out in a police cell that his father was an admiral; naturally no one believed him and he was returned under escort to the *Dido* next morning to be punished with a few days' stoppage of leave.

We sailed at noon; the *Dido* for Casablanca, the *Duke of York* for Villefranche.

The trouble with being young and trying to write, is other writers. Whatever you've been reading last gets between author and object, producing a solemn and ineffective pastiche, and so it was in my case. 'Going abroad' seemed to me so significant that I had begun to keep a journal (which doubled as letters to my mother) and which, however useful to me now as an aid to memory, has caused me nothing but acute embarrassment on re-reading and even from time to time a physical blush. The Surrealist declamatory style covered any revolutionary or poetic statements but, when it came to description, my current model was Cyril Connolly's *Unquiet Grave*, a book then recently published, which had impressed me both deeply and disastrously.

'We sailed for Villefranche [I wrote]. The blood soon moves with the sea. We arrived in the morning: mountains, the sleeping villas of the rich and the town on the quay. The seduction of colour: violet, white, pink, lemon, blue, green and scarlet. The seduction of heat, the wish to become a plant, to grow roots, vegetate and decay.'

Ashore, Tom and I had several adventures. On our first leave, in a little bar as evening was falling, an enormous woman and her seven-year-old daughter came in. The child, who carried a marigold, was affected in the extreme. She told us she was a queen, strutted like a peacock, scratched herself like a monkey, offered us her hand to kiss and stuck her fingers in the air shrieking with manic laughter. Her mother smiled fondly, showing discoloured teeth. She told us her daughter's name was Monique. Later, after omelettes, Camembert, French bread, red wine and coffee, feeling very much men of the world, smoking Gauloises and trying out our deplorable French on the *patron*, Monique was taken upstairs to be put to bed and immediately the *patron* intimated, a finger laid alongside his tapir-like nose, that if we waited the mother would return. This news froze us with horror but we could think of no way to escape.

The woman came in. Before she had smelt strongly of sweat. Now it was of sweat and cheap but pungent scent. She was not alone either. With her was another elderly whore, but bony and angular where she was fat and greasy. We bought them drinks, hoping to delay or avoid any further move. They nibbled our ears and ran down the Americans, whom they claimed were not *gentils*. They asked us if the English were as 'cold' as popular French legend maintained. We were in a quandary there: too enthusiastic a denial would only precipitate matters, but national pride demanded some defence. This, mild as it was, brought on the crisis. They led us into a back room where there was a divan, a brass bed and a portable bidet. On the discoloured walls was an Edwardian print of a naked woman with enormous thighs and buttocks. The fat *putain*, not unlike this image if considerably less fetching, reclined on the divan and patted a place for me to sit on it. The skeletal hag began to pull the petrified Tom towards the dubious bed. An inspiration, conceived in panic, struck me. I looked at my watch and clapped my hand against my brow in an exaggeratedly histrionic manner. The charm of their company had made me forget the time. We must catch the last bus back into Villefranche. Both women protested noisily, but I was firm. We would return on Monday. Slightly mollified they insisted on seeing us to our bus. There, under the cynical eye of a Petty Officer from the *Duke*, they embraced us fervently.

The next time Tom and I went ashore we decided to visit Monte Carlo, but before we left the harbour I was arrested by the French Customs. Cigarettes and soap were in very short supply in France that spring of 1947, and, like most of the ship's company, I had thought it worth the risk to smuggle. So carelessly had I planted these commodities about me that, while I was buying a stick of nougat at a stall, a plain-clothed official, after the most casual glance at my bulging person, signalled to a uniformed colleague, tapped me on the shoulder, and told me to accompany them.

In the cool Customs shed I decided the best thing was to come clean. I put everything down on the long trestle table, and they demanded an explanation. I told them they were all for my mistress in Monte Carlo. She smoked like a chimney. And the soap? Very necessary *après l'amour*. They smiled. I took the opportunity to slide two packets of Gold Flakes away from the others and towards them. I carefully didn't look in that direction. The packets vanished. They said I could go, and showed me how to stow away the soap and the rest of the cigarettes more convincingly. The thing was, they told me, that some sailors smuggled things ashore to sell on the black market. *'Deplorable!'* I agreed in my absurd French accent accompanied by exaggerated Gallic gestures. *'Absolument deplorable!'* I think it was my ham acting that made them spare me.

Tom was waiting nervously for me at the bus stop. As the queue was very long and there was no sign of a bus we decided to hitch-hike. Tom was at his worst, bullying me about everything both personal and political until I lost my temper and threw his hat into a public flower bed.

In a café we talked to a boy from Paris. He told me he was an Existentialist, but then most young Frenchmen with any intellectual pretensions claimed to be that in 1947. As Breton and Sartre were at it hammer and tongs I felt obliged, despite my secret admiration for the recently published *Age of Reason*, to defend Surrealism. He brushed this aside with that air of superiority and infallibility of which French youth has always had the secret, dismissing Breton as only interested in external phenomena. If he had been less beautiful, I might well have lost my temper. As it was I asked him to come on board the next day when the *Duke of York* was to be open to visitors.

Leaving him on comparatively amicable terms we set off in the direction of Monte Carlo and eventually we were given a lift by two elderly English ladies who were driving into the principality to shop. They were clearly very rich and told us how relieved they were that the war was over and they could return to live abroad, especially now that the Socialists had taken over and were making life impossible in England. Tom and I knew better than to disagree and anyway, as Anarchists, we felt under no obligation to defend Attlee. I did wonder though what Felix would have done. Probably he would have insisted on getting out and walking, especially if he'd had a few drinks.

Far below us lay the *Duke of York* at anchor. 'A fine life,' said one of the old trouts. They dropped us outside the casino.

I fell immediately and guiltily in love with Monte Carlo. I argued with Tom that if it represented a bad system, it was surely to be superseded by a worse. At least pleasure was involved whereas the grey conformity to come . . . I looked at the policemen in their musical comedy uniforms, the cab horses in their little coats. In the shops were unbelievable luxuries to my war-starved eyes: scent bottles in the shape of medieval towers, lips or stars, orchids streaked with strange colours, huge boxes of chocolates compared with which David Webster's offering looked like a packet of jelly babies.

Men in uniform were not allowed inside the casino, but we bribed an official with some of the cigarettes I'd brought ashore – for following my arrest I hadn't found the courage to try and sell them in Villefranche – and he showed us round. I was particularly impressed by the little theatre. Its gilt and velvet, cherubs and sways of carved fruit seemed the epitome of Edwardian opulence. I would return here with Edouard, I promised myself. I knew he adored the tables and had, several times in his life, faced ruin through his passion for gambling. He had once shown me a photograph of himself strolling along the seafront with a mistress in the 1920s, very much the *boulevardier* with his Maurice Chevalier straw hat and cane.

Short of funds, I suggested to Tom that we went into the most expensive hotel to see if anyone picked us up for dinner. Surprisingly he agreed, aware no doubt that if there was any carnal price to be paid I would do the paying. At the long white bar of the Hotel de Paris I ordered two martinis. 'They are paid for,' said the barman, sleek as a worldly prelate, but it was no rich queen who sidled up to us. Our benefactor was an ex-naval Captain, a loveable old bore abrim with breezy anecdotes. He invited us to join him for dinner – 'Now I don't want you to refuse, lads. Wouldn't ask you if I couldn't afford it!' – and introduced us to a smart, bored woman in her late thirties – 'Runs one of me businesses.' A little later her mother appeared, a dear old thing whose sole contribution to the conversation was to divide everything – people, objects, dishes, décor, politics, places – into one of two classes: 'nice' or 'not nice'.

The Captain took us to a small but expensive restaurant. Tom clammed up completely, but it didn't really matter as our host ranged the seven seas and some forty years afloat on them, while his business associate contributed a certain amount of contemporary scandal. She told us that in their hotel was an ex-mistress of a French duke who brought back a different impossible man every night, but even the servants treated her with contempt! Her mother didn't think this was at all nice. The Captain offered no comment, but went booming on about destroyers during 'the first show'.

After dinner they went to a boxing match and we to the station, Tom complaining bitterly at the boredom of the meal and attacking me for playing up to them. I found this a bit tough as he hadn't exactly held back on either food or drink and had left me to show interest and gratitude. While waiting for the liberty boat we drank green chartreuse and I sent off a letter to E.L.T. There was a lot of flirtatious *entente cordiale* on the jetty between some French and British sailors. Next day the French boy came aboard as promised and I showed him over the ship. In the chain-locker flat where I had taken him, not innocently, but without much hope, he suddenly made a pass at me, and for half an hour the disciples of Jean Paul Sartre and André Breton forgot their differences in each other's arms.

Chapter 11

Before returning to Gibraltar we moved out into the Atlantic for some more manoeuvres. Passing another mess deck I was un-expectedly seized, debagged and had some jam shoved up my arse to the accompaniment of excited and humourless laughter. As a public schoolboy I took this fairly philosophically, reflecting that after all it could have been boot polish for starters, but it led me to think about what I really felt about the Lower Deck and this was easier to do on the huge impersonal *Duke of York* with its wearying and complicated routine, and its inflexible bullshit. My jam besmearing was fortuitous, or, if not so, no more than the result of my advertised effeminacy. I looked coolly that evening at my messmates. There was only Tom I was close to, and our friendship was constantly under strain. For the rest I admired our Leading Seaman, the very funny, astute, humane and well-informed Bill Rainbow. There were three other ratings who seemed to me to have an instinctive grasp of life. They were under-educated, but unblinkered by prejudice or convention. For the rest, I thought, they were all babies, mental age about five and with no curiosity or wish to grow up. The only difference between them was that some were nice babies and some nasty. It was true that most of them were tolerant and easy-going, but there were times, especially when I was over-tired, when the monotony of their conversation, the squabbling over rations, the endless sexual badinage and the senseless and sexless reiteration of rhythmic swear words, drove me almost distraught with irritation. By a chance remark of mine, I discovered that two-thirds of them had never heard of Bernard Shaw. This really surprised me as he was always in the newspapers, frequently to be seen prancing about in his tweeds and bathing-suit on the newsreels, and two of his plays had been made into comparatively successful films. I looked at my messmates with almost Fascist contempt that evening. Perhaps the jam had upset me more than I realized. One boy was writing a letter to a girl he'd met in Portsmouth, quite liked, but wished to make clear that he didn't want her to think he intended to go steady. He asked my advice. Would it be better, with this in mind, to finish up his letter with 'God bless' or 'cheerio'? I said I didn't see it mattered. The mess deck rocked with scorn. 'I thought you were meant to be fucking educated!' said the letter-writer. 'Of course it fucking matters!' The general consensus was that 'cheerio' was less com-mitting and I sulkily slung my hammock.

Arriving back in Gibraltar we discovered that my money for the Spanish trip hadn't arrived and nor had either of our parcels of civilian clothes. We solved the first problem by going aboard the Dido and, as no one had any money to lend us, cashing a cheque with the chaplain. The clothes presented a more serious problem as the one condition the Spaniards had made was that nobody, neither officers nor men, was to wear a uniform. I solved it with the aid of a friend in the clothing store. Some time before the Navy had ordered an alternative working rig, but decided against issuing it. It was to have been called 'Number Eights' and consisted of non-bellbottomed canvas trousers and pale blue shirts. In the stores there were also a number of canary yellow ties of unknown significance and some badgeless red parachute berets. Tom and I tried these outfits on, 'borrowing' them in exchange for a ration of tickler and the promise of both our tots before dinner. Personally, I thought we looked rather dashing.

The next morning, when it was still misty, with the promise of heat, we climbed excitedly into the cutter and were rowed across the calm waters of the harbour to where the officers and ratings in their 'civvies' were waiting to board the coaches into Spain. There were comparatively few ratings who'd decided to go but amongst them were Felix and the 'orrible Peter Ward. Felix was at first effusively friendly to me (less so to Tom whom he had not forgiven for half-accidentally cutting his nose the night we got so drunk in Gibraltar), but suddenly, after a few words from Peter, he became inexplicably cold and distant. When Peter had gone off for a pee, I asked him what it was all about and, rather shamefacedly, he told me. Peter had insisted, and Felix had agreed, that as they were to be in civilian clothes, they must look smarter than any of the officers; a revenge aimed to compensate for Peter's irritation at being ordered about by men he privately considered extremely common but whose uniform entitled them to treat him as an inferior. In consequence, both had gone to immense trouble. Peter was in a very well-cut suit in Prince of Wales check and looked as if on his way to a rather smart race meeting. Felix presented an equally impressive if rather more rural image in good but excessively hairy tweeds and shoes heavy enough for rough shooting. The officers in their off-the-pegs, blue blazers and grey flannels were indeed, in the most literal terms, out-classed. Peter's rage and Felix's coldness (for despite his many true qualities he was not entirely displeased to be chosen out of the entire ship's company as the only possible companion by the son of an earl) was due to finding their one-up-manship ruined by having to acknowledge two figures dressed like the opening song-and-dance act on a third-rate music-hall bill.

Two coaches were waiting, but what with all the sulking and

furtive explanations going on, we were rather late finding seats. Somehow (I forgot if I engineered it or not), I found myself on the same coach as Felix and Peter with Tom sitting by the driver in the other one. Accident or no, I was disgracefully relieved. Without Tom's aggressive intransigence, I could at least bring Peter round to the point of toleration — not, to be fair to myself, that I cared all *that* much about his good opinion, but I was desperate to regain the right to Felix's company, without whose jokes and cultural cross references I felt the trip would lose much of its zest. As an initial tender of my good intentions I removed my tie and beret and put them in my ditty box, promising to buy a more suitable tie at our first stop. Felix's naturally gregarious and affectionate disposition soon surfaced but Peter still sulked. 'I won't have lunch with you!' he snapped.

The coaches moved across no-man's-land towards the heavily-guarded frontier, containing this microcosm of the great British obsession with class structure. To recap in more general terms: an aristocrat and a member of the upper-middle classes having dressed up in order to demonstrate the social inferiority of their middle-class naval superiors are betrayed by the appearance of a couple, one middle class, the other educated working class, the former of which is prepared to disassociate himself from the latter in order to regain the attention of the member of the upper-middle classes, who is himself unwilling to relinquish the approval of the aristocrat. At the same time I was equally obsessed with Spain, as of course were Felix and the betrayed Tom. Here entirely different cultural criteria were at work: Egalitarianism, Revolution, Anarchy! How the mind is able, admittedly more often when one is young, to accept two simultaneous concepts which not only bear no relation to each other but furthermore demand totally different responses has remained a continuous puzzle to me. I glared with loathing at the soldiers at the border in their 'dung coloured uniforms', shook with fervent indignation as an officer stopped an old peasant with a donkey and, having emptied the paniers full of rags and papers on to the dusty ground, stirred them over with his jack-boot and strode off. I inwardly cursed the policemen in their coal-scuttle hats and cloaks, and blessed the impassive peasantry in whose heart, I was sure, still smouldered that revolutionary spark which would one day burst into glorious flame.

We moved on into Andalusia, Felix and I quoting Auden at each other, and wondering – wrongly as it happens – if Cyril Connolly, Spender or Isherwood had passed along this way a decade earlier. Peter asked who on earth these people were. 'Poets,' we told him. 'Writers,' he snorted with the contemptuous indignation of the confirmed philistine. I'd achieved my object. Felix would never isolate himself for two days with someone who'd never heard of Auden.

In retrospect it is amazing just how much that poet did mean to people of my generation and temperament, He was of course a great poet, but I think there was more to it than that. My own belief is that he was able to express our revolutionary aspirations while at the same time indicating that he shared our background and our guilty love/hate for its way of life and institutions; a spiritual nanny to bandage our knees and warm the milk for our Ovaltine after our imaginary struggles on the barricades. Even when prophesying the collapse of capitalism, he made its decay wistfully attractive and there was, in his stern admonitions, something reassuringly reminiscent of a popular and fair-minded head of the house telling one off for slacking. Even the phrase for which he has been so often and so severely attacked, 'the necessary murder', had no more weight than 'the necessary beating' which would hurt him more than it hurt you, but was essential for the sake of the school.

This is not a recantation. The younger Auden was infinitely superior to the drunken and dribbling reactionary of the later years, and Fascist Spain remained, up to the death of Franco, indeed up to the time of writing, a repressive and brutal regime. Speaking as an Anarchist, I held even then no illusions about Stalinist Communism or indeed any other kind. What I regret though is the way I couldn't look at what I saw without interpreting it through a grid. If one learns anything as one gets older, and sadly one forgets a lot too, it is to objectify.

The trip involved a visit to a sherry factory on the estate of a marquis. By the gates were two wire cages, one containing budgerigars, the other crocodiles. As it was siesta time the tall white buildings were deserted. In the sunny yards were trees of bitter Seville oranges. We walked between the great vats of maturing sherry, past armies of bottles and through the yard where the barrels were made. The guide told us they were made from real American oak, and that is was very expensive. Finally we came to a cleared space at the end of one of the buildings. Here was a long trestle table on which were dishes of stuffed olives, bits of cheese, anchovies and rusks. Girls in Andalusian costumes offered us sherry, glass after glass of it and pretended that they were unable to understand the word 'no'. We, for our part, pretended that we minded. Swigging it back, I sententiously suggested to Felix that it was clear that the Government wished us to see the country 'through an alcoholic mist'. Equally solemnly he stopped drinking long enough to agree.

On the ends of some huge casks which lined the walls were photographs of previous marquises. In one of them the present owner, as a small boy wearing a straw hat, was playing with a toy sherry barrel. A little later he appeared in person, and stood there, plump, sleek, and smiling blandly, as he watched us lurching about. On leaving we were presented with three sample bottles of sherry and a big bottle of Spanish brandy. If my conjecture as to the intentions of the Spanish Government was in any way justified, we were certainly co-operating most whole-heartedly.

We lunched in Jerez at a hotel where the page-boys insisted on shaking hands. I remember walking about the lobby arm in arm with one, but as everybody was so drunk it seemed in no way indiscreet or even mildly unconventional. Lunch was a disaster. Most of the ratings were 'flakers' in the lavatory and the *Dido*'s doctor was constantly interrupted. Although by this time I could have joined Felix and Peter, I decided not to, believing it would serve as a mild slap across the wrist to Felix, and sat down with another rating off the *Dido*. It was as well I did so. The rating vanished precipitously between the *hors d'oeuvres* and the two fried eggs which followed it, and simultaneously Tom appeared, roaring drunk and in no mood to avoid a confrontation with the 'orrible Peter Ward, which would have carried us all back to square one.

Tom's bus had visited a different factory, which had given them just as much to drink and nothing at all to eat and, although he carried on from where the other rating had left off, it wasn't enough to settle the sherry and he was violently sick afterwards.

After lunch I wandered through the town like a somnabulist Pied Piper pursued by a great number of children, for I had foolishly given one of them a small coin. They were dressed in rags, pitifully thin and their hair was shaved close to their skulls, which were covered with scabs and bald patches. On returning to the coaches, Felix took a photograph of Tom and myself surrounded by these waifs, all of them, I must admit, grinning like demons.

Between Jerez and Seville we slept. In a letter to my mother I explained that this was because 'the country was flat and dull'. I suspect that even if we had been crossing the most dramatic and romantic terrain in Europe, we would have slept just the same. In the suburbs, passing a San Francisco convent, Peter suddenly and uncharacteristically burst into song:

'San Francisco,
Open your golden gates,
Never a stranger waits,
Outside your door!'

I took this to be a sign that he was mellowing. Felix did too. He gave me a conspirational wink. I was right, and with Felix and me acting as buffer states, Peter and Tom found it just about possible to co-exist for the rest of the tour.

The Spanish authorities did us pretty well for our six pounds. They put us up in Seville at the Hotel Madrid, which I found enchanting. There was a courtyard full of plants and weathered statues. The floors were tiled. Very old maids tottered about their duties wearing uniforms of an Edwardian formality, and in the corridors, on the darkly papered walls, were huge elaborately framed nineteenth-century academic pictures: lionesses suckled their young, seas of treacle crashed on cardboard rocks, paper flowers burgeoned, wooden parrots preened. Over the reception desk was the official photograph of the Generalissimo, and here and there, about the passages, statues of saints and many examples of what I had learnt to think of as '*cet objet-là*' – the crucifix.

The reason I called the crucifix '*cet objet-là*' was the result of a story Edouard had told me about a quarrel between Breton and Magritte just before Magritte returned to Brussels from Paris at the beginning of the 1930s. Magritte and his wife Georgette went to a Surrealist séance in a Monmartre café and Georgette (possibly put up to it by René, who was by no means devoid of mischief) was wearing a crucifix which had belonged to her mother. On seeing this Breton, whose atheism was of a religious intensity, started back like a vampire in the same situation, demanding to know why and by what right Madame Magritte should come to a Surrealist meeting wearing (and he pointed towards it) *cet objet-là!* Magritte took it very coolly. It was her mother's. What did it matter? She was fond of it. Breton persisted in his indignation. The Magrittes left the café. René's independence of spirit was too real to yield to Breton. He remained a Surrealist certainly, but at a distance.

I loved this story and made Mesens tell me it many times but, as a convinced atheist and having no love for the sado-masochistic symbol of Christianity, I found it very amusing to refer to the crucifix at all times as '*cet objet-là*', although not without awareness that there was, within Breton, a certain pedantic exactitude bordering on the absurd, and that this was part of the joke.

Some time before dinner Felix and the mollified Peter came to our room and we drank lots of brandy out of tooth mugs. Things went smoothly enough for us to eat together and we discussed sexual deviation. Tom took no part in the conversation – he was sulking because he'd been forced to wear a tie – but Peter adopted the duty stallion attitude: screwing girls was all right, anything else perfectly disgusting. Felix and I spoke up for inclination. If a man falls in love with a stag that is his (and the stag's) affair, the only wrong was to believe there was anything superior about it. What we were really doing of course was talking about our own feelings under the cover of a theoretical discussion. Not that in my case stags came into it, but the young waiter did.

By the end of the dinner we were quite drunk again and Peter's heterosexuality had won us round sufficiently to produce general enthusiasm at the idea of a visit to a brothel. He had quite a lot of money, he said, and would stake us. We could pay him back later. We looked up the Spanish for brothel in Felix's handy phrasebook where, rather to our surprise, it was listed, and we tumbled out into the street. After asking several men who looked as if they might visit brothels but who in fact rejected our enquiry quite crossly, we got into a taxi. The man, leering at us intermittently, drove dangerously down several tortuous side streets and dropped us outside a considerable house. We were let in by an old woman dressed in rusty black and wearing a silver 'cet objet-là' round her wrinkled neck. She showed us into a room with stuffed bulls' heads on the dark green walls. Around the table sat the girls, all quite pretty and chattering away like budgies. With them sat the boss, a mild-looking old man wearing a beret. He greeted us ceremoniously. The old woman quoted her prices, scribbling them down on a piece of paper to make certain we understood. Suddenly Peter announced that, after all, he had no money and the rest of us burst into relieved giggles. I suppose we would have gone through with it, but I remember being secretly delighted we didn't have to. It took some time to convince madame that we were not, after all, punters; she clearly thought we were simply haggling and kept making reductions on her piece of paper; but finally she understood. Everyone took it quite calmly, the girls asked for cigarettes. We sat smiling at them for some time and then, with noisy bravado, left. Out in the street we all turned on Peter, hypocritically pretending to be frightfully disappointed, but soon after we found ourselves in a bar, Peter's money mysteriously rematerialized and we drank ourselves legless on Spanish brandy.

I have no recollection of going back to the hotel but woke, with a monster hangover, to find a basin full of vomit on the surface of which floated a cigar stub and a dead carnation. While

I was trying to unblock the sink with the stalk of the flower, the phone rang. 'This is the manager,' it said. 'Your be'aviour last night was hay disgrace. I shall 'ave to hask you to leave the 'otel.' With visions of court martial if this were to become known, I barked back with all the authority I could muster that he must be mistaken, and asked him to come and see me in my room in ten minutes. There was a giggle on the other end of the line. It was Felix. Later he confessed that he, in his turn, had been worried. So convincing was my bluster that he feared he might have got on to a Lieutenant Commander's room by mistake.

The drain unblocked and rinsed, I took a bath and tottered down to breakfast feeling as fragile as a piece of Dresden.

'Is this all we get?' growled a Lieutenant at the next table as they served us coffee and rolls in the pale sunlight of the court-yard. I allowed myself a world-weary smile. The Mesens had taught me to accept the idea of continental breakfast. I didn't even admit to myself that like the Lieutenant I'd much sooner have tucked into bacon and eggs.

Two sailors, looking very much the worse for wear, staggered in off the street and sat down. I knew one of them slightly and asked what he'd been up to. He leered triumphantly and slapped the back of his neck several times; a Lower Deck piece of mime representing sexual congress. The surrounding officers glared at him like figures in an H. M. Bateman cartoon. He suddenly realized where he was and, blushing furiously, mumbled an apology.

Tom hadn't surfaced for breakfast but as I was on my way upstairs to pack, the Lieutenant who had complained about his breakfast called me over. I felt very worried for a moment, believing that perhaps after all Felix's joke had some basis in reality, but it was all right.

'Would you pass it on to the chaps,' he said, 'not to get so drunk today. The point is they think you're all naval officers so don't let the side down. We want to get the most out of it of course and have a jolly good time and all that, but yesterday several people passed out and that's really not on. So pass it on eh, there's a good chap.'

I said I would, having no intention of doing so. I resented his assumption that, just because I'd been to a public school, I was prepared to act as prefect to his house master. In the hall, under the photograph of the Generalissimo, I wrote postcards to Edouard and Reggie and stuck smaller versions of the same image on each of them. I've always been puzzled that dictators, or come to that kings and presidents, choose to have their portrait on stamps to be licked with the tongues and bunged into place with the fists of their subjects. It doesn't do them any harm of course, but nor is it very respectful. I gave Franco a good double thumping.

It was time to sight-see. Tom was unwashed, stale-pissed and very irritating. Peter was at his most affable. It had begun to drizzle. The orange trees glowed in the damp air. Jose, the guide, said we must wait for the Father who was to show us over the cathedral. I was delighted he was late, plump, and very short of breath. As soon as he was on the bus Tom announced he had to go for a piss.

'Hurry up,' hissed Peter, seething with irritation. I was disloyally pleased by Tom's angry discomfiture.

When he did get back the bus wouldn't start anyway, so we had to walk through the fine rain. Seville seemed more austere than I'd imagined, but there were statues and fountains, tiled pavements and palm trees – we were abroad all right.

Given my intransigent atheism it may come as a surprise that I was prepared to enter a cathedral, but I had rationalized that some time before, and even tried out my solution on E.L.T., who had given me an official (Surrealist) dispensation. Church parades apart, and I was soon to do something about that, I swore I would never go into a church for an overt act of worship; a resolution I kept until my father died in 1961 when, unlike Joyce's Stephen Daedalus, I broke my vow for my mother's sake, and having done it once without shaking my non-faith, have been to several weddings and funerals since. At the time, I argued that churches were also museums and the repositories of treasure. To treat them as such and nothing else was no betrayal. One didn't after all concede anything to their spiritual claims. With this rubric to still my conscience, I followed the plump little priest into the great early Gothic edifice.

No nave leading up to the high altar, I noted with the disapproval of an ex-Protestant communicant. Private chapels all round the walls and a great cluster of them in the centre, each with a saint or 'cet objet-là' illuminated by a plantation of candles flickering and guttering. The statues varied a great deal; some were like Victorian wax dolls, others like Gothic carvings. There was one larger chapel in High Baroque, marble and gilt with Doric columns.

'Here hall the 'igh class peoples his married,' said the Father, showing his bad teeth. 'General Franco's daughter his married here.'

There were pictures in some of the chapels, but coated with heavy brown varnish and difficult to see through the railings. There was a Murillo, a painter I've always disliked anyway: a saint rolling up his eyes to heaven at a cherub as vulgar as Disney. Here and there were huge pop-eyed figures used in carnivals which secretly, as an ex-C. of E. worshipper, I found rather a shocking idea. The same was true of the information, handed out by the priest in the most casual way, that on certain feast days the choirboys, dressed in scarlet surplices, danced, accompanying themselves on castanets, on the steps of the altars. Nothing like that ever happened in Christ Church, Linnet Lane, Liverpool 17, or the chapel at Stowe School, Bucks. It sounded extremely frivolous.

I was reassured when a bell rang, and the old cleaning women stopped scrubbing the pavements, crossed themselves and prayed devoutly until another bell released them to continue their work with renewed vigour. There was proof of Pavlovian conditioning and holy brainwashing. Despite the dancing and pop-eyed carnival grotesques there was power here and religio-political horse trading. Franco was a devout Catholic and, in exchange, the Church were good Fascists. It had stopped raining when I came out, with a keen sense of release, into the Cathedral Square. I asked Felix if I was right and he reassured me that I was. The Church, he said in his measured and considered way, was perhaps the strongest factor in winning the war for the Falangists. Peter looked irritated and puzzled. Church for him was where you went in the country or, if in London, for baptisms, weddings, funerals and memorial services. What were we making such a fuss about?

We went over to the Alcazar, built by the Moorish Emirs and later taken over by the Spanish king, who added a second storey. No crisis of conscience here. I walked confidently through the court and rooms proclaiming it self-evident that such fine proportions, such restrained and refined intricacy, could only be the fruits of an advanced civilization. I chose to ignore, or perhaps at that time didn't even know, that the most hideous atrocities of the Spanish Civil War had been perpetrated, admittedly in the service of Christian Franco, by his Moorish troops. The Spanish floor was a splendid junkshop of many periods. The pictures in particular were deliciously bad. There was one enormous painting of a solemn nineteenth-century couple looking at a fountain representing a pissing horse. There was also an ornate billiard room presented by Edward VII and preserved intact.

Franco, the guide told us, had helped with the restoration of the exterior. 'Franco, he come. He say, "What's be'ind this wall?" They say, "Hay Moorish wall, sir." He say, "Take down this wall".' I tried to find something discreditable in the story but failed.

It was nearly lunch time and Felix and I went off together to have an aperitif. This was not difficult as Tom wasn't speaking to anyone, and Peter was still irritated by my hysteria and Felix's don-like analysis of the links between Fascism and Catholicism. We had sat down in a square, sipping white wine, nibbling olives and little bits of raw fish, when some men approached and offered us a shoe-shine. We accepted. The sun shone. We were content. Before we were aware of it, the shoe-shine men had pulled off our heels, replaced them with new ones, and were demanding the equivalent of eight shillings each. How did the Anarchist and Socialist react to this? Did we accept it, even welcome it as a sign of the ability to revolt even under the most oppressive regime? We did not! Pretending that he had to change a note Felix hurried off to look for Jose. I remained, trying to appear impassive under the suspicious eyes of our opponents. It took Felix twenty long minutes to locate the guide but when he did there was an almighty rumpus, involving not only our assailants and our champion but swelling rapidly to include many passers-by, some of our party, some of theirs. Eventually Jose reached a compromise. We must pay four shillings each. With bad and blimpish grace we did so. On the way to lunch Jose launched into another of his worryingly neutral stories.

'These men, they cheat hanyone – even Spanish peoples. A friend hof mine meet a man. He say, "Hi ham the gardener hof the Bishop hof Seville. Hi sell you some seeds hof the most beautiful carnations hin the world." My friend buy them, he plant them and hup come not one carnation! Just hay lot hof dirty grass!!!'

I didn't even try to find an anti-Fascist moral in this one.

After lunch we climbed into the buses for the long drive back. After Jerez it grew darker. We finished the brandy. Felix and I chatted quietly as the bus drove on. The last light died on the hills. We crossed the border and parted on the quay. We swore that if, after our demob, there was an uprising we would go and fight. We were not to be put to the test, of course. Franco died in 1975 in the same hospital as a man dreadfully tortured by his police.

At noon next day I watched the *Dido* steam past with some envy and irritation. It was en route for Casablanca, which to me, as a lover of Bogart films, was sacred ground. We, on the other hand, were bound for Madeira. It took two days and, as the harbour wasn't big enough to accomodate a battleship, we anchored some distance off shore. On arrival little boats, manned by bare-footed Portuguese of piratical appearance, rowed out to barter wicker furniture and needle-boxes, and stalks of green bananas, a fruit unseen in England since the second year of the war. The ship's tannoy warned us that trading was forbidden, but gazing over the side I could see jerseys and seaboots furtively passing out through the portholes of the Lower Deck. It was a cold day and the boys who dived for pennies hugged their bronzed bodies and shivered.

Tom went ashore the next day but I decided not to. By morning a ground swell had arisen and didn't die down until the day before we left. There was no leave as it was too rough for the liberty boats and so I never got ashore at all, whereas Tom was stranded for three happy days and crowed about it non-stop on his return. Our relationship had by now soured into almost continuous bickering and was never really to recover for more than an hour or two at a time.

We sailed for Portland, the first few days in hot sun with everybody off duty sunbathing on the deck. While we'd been away England had experienced one of the coldest winters of the century and as we approached the Channel it was back to heavy sea jersies under the cold grey skies. Despite the weather I was in high spirits. In three days Tom and I were to return to the *Dido*. It's true I had fourteen days' stoppage of leave for losing my paybook but, as I'd hoped, when we were transferred the RPO scribbled out the punishment. I rushed happily away to find the Baron, Edward Wood, Felix and the 'orrible Peter Ward, all very friendly and larger than life on the dear little ship. The next day we were sailing back to Chatham and in a fortnight's time leave. Nothing could spoil my pleasure, but one unfriendly eye was watching me, determined to do its best. Warrant Officer Perkins was biding his time.

Chapter 12

Warrant Officer Perkins' first opportunity wasn't long in coming although in the event he muffed it, a setback that made him all the more determined. I had assiduously cultivated an artistic reputation on the *Dido*, sitting on the deck sketching the harbour, or going ashore with sketchbooks and paints to turn out fairly competent if completely unoriginal gouaches of where-ever we happened to be. My motivation was not entirely affected, I genuinely enjoyed sketching, but I discovered that there were side-advantages too. Any job which required some painting skill, ship's posters for example, fell my way. There was the time too when the British Council (there was as yet no Arts Council) sent to the *Dido*, for the edification of the boy seamen who were expected to be given a certain amount of general education, a series of large boards on which were photographs and reproductions comparing African sculpture with Cubist painting. There were some notes provided but this somewhat esoteric subject was not part of the schoolie's armoury and, having satisfied the Commander as to my competence, I spent a pleasant afternoon while everybody else was on deck doing something freezing and boring, explaining to the admittedly indifferent boy seamen (including the one with skin like a wardroom plate) how the masks and fetishes of the Ivory Coast and the French Congo were more important than Cezanne in the development of Braque and Picasso, a theory I had assimilated from E. L. T. Mesens.

When we arrived at Chatham the Captain decided to hold a cocktail party for the senior officers of the Home Fleet on their return from the Mediterranean cruise. The Commander suggested I be commissioned to paint a large mural to hang between the guns on the quarterdeck and I proposed a mock early sea map, with mermaids and monsters and humorous illustrations of the places we'd visited. This was accepted and for several days I toiled pleasantly at the work. On Gibraltar I placed the three wise monkeys wearing naval officers' caps and at Villefranche sailors and tarts (the Commander asked me to move the position of one of the matelot's hands). It was finished in time and hung in its place looking, I had to admit, quite decorative. It was something of a success, a talking-point, and, when the party had been going on for some time and a great deal of gin been taken, I was sent for by the proud Commander and made much of. I was also given far too much to drink and, by the time I staggered down to the mess deck, my first optimistic reaction to the alcoholic excess had turned lachrymose and revolutionary. It was past Lights Out but I was determined to persuade my grumbling shipmates that the triumph of Anarchism was over-due. Standing on a mess table and speaking, for some incomprehensible reason, in a strong German accent, I appealed for them to shed their chains. The noise I was making attracted the attention of my enemy and he came below to find out who was responsible. Luckily another stage was imminent. Revolutionary fervour was about to yield to nausea. Hanging on to one of the bars from which we slung our hammocks I was sick mostly over his shoes. He grinned like a wolf; I could see his features clearly in between the waves of approaching unconsciousness.

'Leading Seaman,' he said with deceptive mildness, 'this man is drunk and I hold you responsible. He's on a charge and you too for neglecting your duty. See the mess is cleared up immediately.'

The Leading Seaman said he would do as ordered but, if he might be allowed to say so, he felt it inadvisable. Perkins coloured and told him, with menacing calm, to explain himself. The Leading Seaman did so – undeniably drunk, but made so by the Upper Deck – case likely to be dismissed – mural for cocktail party – hardly likely to make it stick.

The Warrant Officer thought it over, and decided to fight another day. As he left the mess deck, I collapsed and was put into my hammock by the Leading Seaman and a very diverted Baron. I woke with no remembrance of any of this but was told about it at breakfast.

'Watch out for that mongolian shirt Perkins,' advised the Baron. 'He's a right bastard and anyway he's out for your fucking blood now.'

Perkins said nothing more about the incident. I passed him at stand easy in the recreation space and he didn't seem to see me at all. I had no further trouble from him before I went home for Easter leave.

In the middle of my leave the King of Denmark died and we were recalled, as the *Dido* had been chosen to represent the Fleet, and to carry across an elderly admiral and a marine band which was going to play in the funeral procession. The admiral seemed quite a cheery old gentleman, who promenaded the ship most of the day, acknowledging our salutes with bluff panache. Felix, however (and after all he had an inside knowledge of admirals), thought he'd be a bit of a bastard if crossed and we were indeed warned to creep about the ship in the early morning for fear of waking him.

We arrived at Copenhagen at dusk and made fast to the jetty, watched by a large crowd. I was very surprised by how alike the Danes looked: to my eyes they seemed almost as interchangeable as a similar gathering of Chinese. Only one young man stuck out from the rest and he turned out to be a Geordie who had settled there and was soon exchanging what were undoubtedly obscene, but to my ears impenetrable, pleasantries with two stokers from his native Newcastle who were leaning on the gang-rail.

Scrubbing decks early next morning (as quietly as possible for fear of disturbing the admiral) I could see rather more of the place. We were quite close to that banal little mermaid, but on the quay was a statue of a polar bear with two cubs which had a certain kitsch charm. The Baron however didn't think much of it. 'Fuck a bear with birdshit all over its swede,' he said dismissively, and indeed it was almost white with the droppings of the great flocks of pigeons which, rather than the gulls, seemed to have commandeered the dockyard.

Stand easy produced a surprise. Instead of the usual meagre biscuits or soggy fruit cake, there was tray upon tray of Danish pastries and cakes bursting with real cream. How can this be, I asked myself as I wolfed down a second plate from the kiosk in the recreation space. Denmark was occupied and we weren't, and yet, only a year after the end of the war, they've got all the cream cakes they want and we've still got butter rationing. It was a question we were to ask ourselves for several years to come.

That afternoon Felix and Edward were on duty and I was so irritated with Tom I refused to go ashore with him. I asked another rating, an engaging fellow with a weakness for the ballet, and, as he had a date at seven that evening, arranged to meet the Baron at a typical rendezvous – 'Outside the baronial lavatory in the main square at seven o'clock for "big eats".'

The city was cleaner than any I'd encountered before and had dealt with mourning its late King with a certain commercial astuteness. In the window of a parfumerie was a single large white bottle of scent with a black bow round its neck and, in a very chic couturier, a solitary black hat acknowledging the respects of an unaccompanied black shoe.

We went to a modern art show of young Danish painters, very

Expressionist, messy and derivative, but I managed to see some paintings by Munch, whom Edouard had described as 'the Van Gogh of the North'. Then we drank schnapps, which I'd never tried before and found quite extraordinary, exploding like a warm but lethal jellyfish at the back of the nose.

At seven the balletomane went to meet his date, and, rather louchely, I took up my station outside the gents. It was indeed baronial by contemporary British standards, clinically clean and extremely large with its own cloakroom and shoe-shine parlour. As the Baron hadn't shown up by 7.30 p.m. I decided to give up and went into one of the smarter restaurants for dinner. I ordered fish with a rich sauce, half a duck, an ice, and cheese and biscuits. Halfway through the Gargantuan meal I saw the Baron wandering past and ran out to fetch him in. Had I known how drunk he was I'd have hesitated and indeed his carry-on over the next hour will explain why Felix and my other friends refused to go ashore with him.

Explaining that he had spent the afternoon asleep in a park, a statement confirmed by the mud and grass all over his person, he yelled 'Shirt' at the waiter and ordered the duck. This was some time coming but it didn't worry the Baron. First he grabbed a piece of fish that someone had left on their plate at the next table and then, realizing that his behaviour was causing a bad impression with the solid Danish families around us, aggravated the offence by explaining to me very loudly and at some length that they had all, without exception, played with themselves when young. At last the duck arrived and the Baron, having jabbed at it once or twice with a fork, picked it up in both hands and gnawed at it with uninhibited and noisy satisfaction.

As most of the Danes understand English rather well and the Baron in between his shark-like assaults on the duck's carcass continued to accuse them of 'interfering with themselves', a linguistic variation on his previous assertion but no less insulting, I was very relieved when the 'shirt' was summoned and the bill assertively demanded and reluctantly settled.

We walked out without any major disaster and were accosted by an extraordinary-looking child with a grotesquely large head covered with thick golden curls, who offered to lead us to a bar, where Bing and Bong provided the music. Here we got stuck into litres of ice-cold lager and I began to catch the Baron up. At his suggestion I bought a rose from an itinerant flower-seller and presented it to a girl on the other side of the room telling her, with tedious and repetitive gallantry, that she was the Mona Lisa of the twentieth century.

Drink had unloosed the Baron's id and that same beast which had thrown the boiling water over my feet came lumbering out. The Baron produced a dagger and said he wanted to stab some-body. He left the café and I nervously followed him, although how I could have frustrated his murderous intentions if he had persisted I can in no way imagine, unless it was by drawing them on myself. Happily his mood changed again and, after eating several sandwiches from a slot machine, a source of nourishment unknown to me until then, we fell into several other bars and, although the Baron got drunker and drunker, there was no recurrence of his psychotic aspect.

Somewhere I conducted a small orchestra with a bread knife. They were playing *The Flower Waltz*. Somewhere I danced with a girl with a most un-Danishlike complaint – BO. The Baron made friends with a very small American sailor with bright red hair and no chin. They sat together with their arms round each other's necks, spilling their beer and moaning about their respective navies. Eventually I found myself drunkenly proposi-tioning the Mona Lisa of the twentieth century, who had mysteriously reappeared – or was it that we had returned to the original bar, the domain of Bing and Bong? She rejected my advances most gently.

'You are reminding me,' she told me in her sing-song Danish accent, 'of a gay rabbit,' a simile rather more accurate than she was perhaps aware.

Earlier that day I had bought a large Danish Blue cheese and, unexpectedly, hadn't left it anywhere. It may seem strange to the contemporary reader that I should have bought it at all; today Danish Blue is a despised comestible, a sure sign of a provincially unimaginative and usually impoverished cheese board, but in wartime Britain and for some years after there was only one kind of cheese, a sweating and flavourless soap known officially as 'Cheddar' and more generally as 'mousetrap'. I knew therefore that there was little I could take home that would please my family more than a large Danish Blue, creamy and veined within its rough-cast protective rind. It was the thought of my father's delight that kept me in possession of the cheese throughout that long, drunken, peripatetic evening, but as the Baron now declared his intention of slinging his mick and crashing the baronial swede, I decided to accompany him back to the ship and leave the cheese in its box on the gangway in charge of the guard.

Both objects I accomplished; the Baron staggered aboard, the watch accepted the cheese and I turned back towards the city in search of further adventure. As I walked across the quay I could hear, through an open porthole, the tones of 'The Well-tempered Clavichord', a proof that the Baron had reached the mess deck. As to what I still expected of the night I had no firm idea – perhaps the Mona Lisa of the twentieth century had made some vague promise to fob me off. What I finished up with was a ballet dancer in a white mackintosh, a deceptively young man with remarkably bad teeth. His name was Hans and he invited me back to his flat, where he produced a bottle of Madeira, a coincidence which, in my state of heightened alcoholic con-sciousness, seemed disproportionately significant. It was clear he had hoped for rougher trade than I, but we had quite a cosy time and, as the level of the Madeira fell, he became increasingly confidential. He clearly regretted, if for personal reasons, the departure of the occupying forces and he showed me several photographs of handsome young Germans both in and out of uniform affectionately inscribed. I found this perversely fascin-ating, but was even more intrigued when he searched out several propaganda gramophone records made by a German swing band called Mister Charlie, with the lyrics in English. There was one about Churchill. It went:

> 'He helps the Jews
> He's a friend of the USSR

He's here, he's there, he's everywhere,
The man with the big cigar.'

The backing, although a shade ponderous, wasn't too bad, the trumpet player patently influenced by Nat Gonella.

At first light I left Hans, snoring gently, to his dreams of blonde Aryan beasts and caught a tram back to the dockyard. Going back on board I discovered I had precipitated a crisis. The dog watch had forgotten to tell the morning watch about the cheese and they'd been terrified out of their wits, believing it to be a bomb. I apologized, collected it, and went below for breakfast.

After acting out the naval formula for facing the day: a shit, a shower and a shampoo, I changed my socks, pants and nautical tee-shirt, polished my shoes, ironed my silk and went to find Felix and Edward.

We'd put in to see the funeral procession, which meant in effect a day ashore, and off we went. We caught a tram and Felix told us that it was essential we behave. It was, after all, he emphasized, 'a solemn and portentious occasion'. We immediately, including him, began to giggle helplessly. It didn't matter though. Everybody on the train and indeed throughout the city was incredibly cheerful, laughing and joking as though off to a wedding. We passed the Danish Horse Guards on their way to join the procession. In their dusty blue uniforms they looked like the chorus from the touring company of an under-budgeted production of The Student Prince.

On reaching the centre of the city we sat down in a café to an enormous second breakfast and almost missed the procession. A slow march in the street reminded us of why we were not aboard. The coffin was passing on its gun carriage. Our marines, we decided, were as smart and co-ordinated as automatons, the French chic but casual. I hummed a music hall song I'd found on an old 78 record in a junk shop in Weymouth, 'Ain't it grand to be bloomin' well dead!'

Felix admitted, rather shyly, that it was his twenty-first birthday. We went back to the ship. I borrowed some money to take him and Edward out to a celebratory dinner, and we gorged like boa-constrictors and drank like fishes.

The measured strains of Johann Sebastian greeted me as I returned to my mess deck. The Baron was back too, and in good spirits. He had spent the evening, he told me, 'hanging out of a fifteen-year-old party in a tent'. She spoke no English but had apparently expressed her enthusiasm by singing throughout the repetitive phrase 'Hey-bob-a-rebob', a rhythmic cry taken from a recording by Cab Calloway which was very popular at the time.

We sailed in the morning. The passage back was rough and Felix's birthday dinner was lost over the side. We docked in Portsmouth on Saturday morning and I resumed my broken leave.

The cheese was a great success. My father's mother, a forceful old lady, came as usual to Sunday lunch and, on seeing the Danish Blue, was beside herself with envy. She had been brought up by her grandmother on the Cheshire marshes and was given to old-fashioned expletives of an eighteenth-century flavour.

'Dash m' wig!' she snorted. 'Where did you get that cheese?'

From that day on, my father always referred to cheese as 'Dash m' wig'.

My leave over, I returned to the *Dido* and we resumed our purposeless meandering along the south coast until it was time for the summer cruise: a visit to Guernsey followed by a 'goodwill' tour of Scandinavia. It was now spring, and, in recompense for the arctic winter, both warm and beautiful. There was very little to do. We painted ship, skived as much as we could, and envied those who left to be demobbed.

Warrant Officer Perkins decided that it was high time to have another shot at getting me into trouble. As I've mentioned earlier I had stuck on the inside of my locker a reproduction of Magritte's *Le Viol*. Perkins, passing one day when my locker door was open, decided it was obscene and reported me for displaying it. Next day, just before noon, I was sent for by the Commander, who felt obliged to see if the charge was justified. I opened my locker door and, controlling his amusement with some difficulty, he asked me to explain it. I was only too eager to oblige. Did it provoke desire, I asked rhetorically, Lust? Surely not. Compared with the pin-ups on my shipmates' locker doors it was infinitely less aphrodisiac. Magritte's purpose in painting *Le Viol* was . . . I was all set to launch into a lengthy analysis of the painter's intentions when the Commander, with the thought of a pink gin in the wardroom rapidly gaining the ascendancy, cut me short.

'I really don't think, Warrant Officer Perkins, that in this case . . .' I stood there, finding it hard not to register my pleasure at my enemy's discomfiture.

'You may go, Able Seaman Melly.'

'Ordinary Seaman, Sir.'

He looked surprised, asked me how long I had been in the Navy and said he would look in to why I hadn't been promoted. As a result, a week later, with the helpful recommendation of the Leading Seaman of F Mess, I was made an Able Seaman, and back-dated six months with quite a lot of pay. *Le Viol*, much to the indignation of Warrant Officer Perkins, continued to smile hairily if enigmatically at the ship's company every time I opened my locker door.

Despite this shot across my bows, and its unexpectedly helpful outcome, I in no way kept what is now called a low profile. On the contrary I decided to attempt an extremely provocative, and perhaps, up until that time, unprecedented feat: to have the religious denomination on my naval papers altered to 'atheist', and to be given permission not to attend church parade. My reasons for this were part irritation, part genuine conviction, and certainly part exhibitionism. My strategy however was the opposite of Surrealist intransigence. I went to see the chaplain, a reasonable young Welshman with whom I had a rather friendly relationship. To him I put it that as a sincere Christian it was surely as offensive for him to realize that a non-believer was being forced to pay lip-service to what he believed in, as it was for me to pretend to worship something I had no faith in whatsoever. He was entirely convinced by this argument and agreed to be called in my defence when I appeared in front of the Commander on 'requests and defaulters'. It went extremely well and the only concession that I was forced to make was the definition of my non-belief as 'agnostic' rather than 'atheist' which I'd asked for. My papers were solemnly and officially changed – 'Religious Denomination: Agnostic' – and I was excused church parade.

Warrant Officer Perkins, a keen non-conformist, thought to punish me for this impertinence. He told my Chief Petty Officer that, on his orders, I was to clean out the heads (lavatories) during the service. I wasn't taking that lying down. I went screaming to the Chaplain – Wasn't it a further insult to his faith to equate it with cleaning out latrines? He was nearly as angry as I was and went to see the Commander. The order was countermanded and I was free to sit, I must confess smugly, reading the posh papers and listening with some pleasure to the distant singing of Anglican hymns, for which, like Sybil, I had always preserved a nostalgic affection.

The reactions of the ship's company were variable. Predictably the Baron thought it well worthwhile. Despite his love of Johann Sebastian, he was a true iconoclast and the only religious observation I heard him utter was when the tannoy, early one Sunday morning, announced 'Holy Communion on the recreation space', he asked the mess if 'anyone fancied going up for a wet [drink]'. Others, either from conviction or convention, were shocked in varying degrees, the majority were indifferent, but the most surprising reaction came from the ferocious, bearded Master at Arms. Passing his caboosh (small office), once again crowded with woolly animals, I was startled to be called by name.

'I hear,' he said, sewing boot-button eyes on a puce duck, 'that you've had your religious denomination changed to agnostic.'

I explained that I asked to be described as an atheist but had been forced to accept the less definitive description.

'I didn't know,' he said, biting off the thread, 'that you 'ad the intelligence to be fuckin' atheist. Now piss off.'

I went away glowing with that special pleasure which comes from the favourable opinion of someone you fear.

Sex on the *Dido* was comparatively low key but uncensorious.

There were a few obvious homosexuals, the doe-eyed writer for one, many total heterosexuals, and a fair number of those who would, on a casual basis, relieve sexual pressure with their own sex. It was accepted, for instance, on my mess deck, that on Saturday make and mends (half days off) anyone who fancied some mutual masturbation would crash down in the coat locker, a structure of closely-meshed wire like a medium-sized cage. As an open part-time invert I was often solicited on these occasions and usually accepted. Sometimes my masculine role both surprised and disappointed those who had misread my predilections. Mostly, however, it was no problem, and there was as relaxed and tolerant an atmosphere as any I've encountered. I had a sometime affair with a Corporal of the Marines who shared my watch on the quarterdeck, but this was only in the middle watch and mostly, from his point of view anyway, to allay boredom. I think he really preferred our other pastime, which was to raid the officers' galley for bacon, eggs and sausages and fry-up on our electric fire laid dangerously on its back. Sex was not really an issue on the *Dido*. There was much the same atmosphere as at a fairly easy-going public school.

On shore of course the Baron, and those like him, picked up women and, being far from discriminating, would return on board most mornings boasting of some fairly grotesque conquest.

I had resumed diplomatic relations with Tom, but mostly only in respect to our jazz sessions, and I seldom went ashore with him. For Felix, on the other hand, my friendship had grown warmer and I was very pleased, while anchored at Weymouth, when he asked me to go home with him. His father lived in a village not far from Dorchester, a suitable place for his retirement as it was near enough to the sea to add a tang of salt to the air. Here, berthed in an early nineteenth-century Gothic rectory with fine no-nonsense Georgian furniture and portraits of earlier nautical Aylmers on the dining room walls, he was in a position to play squire with stick and spaniel.

'Treacle,' he'd shout at the dog, 'Come here! Here, boy! Heel!' and to the farm labourers, 'Pigs all right, John?'

His wife was like a character out of a play by the then popular dramatist, Esther McCracken, slightly eccentric, rather careless in appearance, given to saying the first thing that came into her head, and extremely kind and easy-going.

There were strawberries and Devonshire cream for tea, sea trout for dinner and, on my first visit, another retired sea-dog and his wife were staying in the house.

'My father's last words,' he told us over the brandy were "for God's sake, m'boy, always dress for dinner" and he was right. It stands for such a lot.'

Felix and I exchanged sardonic glances, resorting to that peculiarly English defense-mechanism by which we can accept what we know to be indefensible. At a village fête the following week our satirical aloofness was put further to the test. Here were feudal privilege, archaic prejudices, forelock tugging, and paternalism rampant, but here too were an organic wholeness, a sense of responsibility and a human scale. Confused by our responses, we concentrated on the more absurd aspects – not that this was difficult.

Through the crackling public address system the local Canon announced the loss of two dogs: 'Such jolly little fellows. One little chap is called Nelson and his brother is Rodney.'

It was evident that Admiral Aylmer was not the only ex-Navy officer to have hove to thereabouts. There were pro-blood sport pamphlets in the temporary lavatory, and almost exaggeratedly Hardyesque rustics in charge of the stalls. Best of all there was a play, acted by the village children with a touching lack of talent and Dorset accents as rich as clotted cream: 'Furry Bluebell, moi dear, oi wonder whurr her Majesty can boie?'

'I find country life a dangerous seduction,' I told Felix on our way back to the *Dido*, and he agreed. Certainly when at home he took on much of the texture of his parents' life, bringing me out what he called 'a stiff whisky to keep the cold out' when I was finishing a sketch in the garden and acknowledging the respectful greetings of the villagers to the manner born. Yet both of us believed in a fairer, more egalitarian society where greetings were an equal acknowledegment of shared humanity and not an outward sign of social status. My own mixed feelings were based on flimsier foundations. My father, despite a lifetime spent of necessity in a Liverpool office, had a yearning for the life of a modest country gentleman, a taste he was only able to fulfil under the aegis of his rich uncles. Most summers they would 'take a place', and round them would gather the more impoverished members of the family to shoot the moors or fish the river. As a child on warm Welsh evenings, beating the pine woods to drive the clattering pigeons towards my father's gun or watching him cast over the river Clwyd, I too fell in love with the idea of such a life. I inwardly envied Admiral Aylmer his ordered life and small domain.

Back aboard, before the summer cruise, there was an audition for a variety concert, one act from each ship, to be given that autumn in front of the King and Queen when they were inspecting the Home Fleet on the Clyde. Sacrificing republican feelings to show-biz I offered 'Frankie and Johnny' and was selected by the chaplain of the *Duke of York*, the Val Parnell of the project, to represent the *Dido*. I was very pleased and wrote immediately to my mother to suggest she come up to Scotland for the occasion. Later I was told that I was not to appear after all, but this lay ahead, and it was in high spirits that we left Portland for a summer cruise, believed to be to Scandinavia, and my last few months in bellbottoms.

Chapter 13

Disappointment awaited us. We were told that we were to visit not, as had been rumoured, Norway and Sweden, but Guernsey and then to return to Chatham. I was not at all thrilled about Guernsey, as it was too English to be thought of as being properly abroad. Nor was I forced to reconsider my prejudice on arrival. The island had been occupied by the Germans and there had been some accusations of fairly widespread collaboration. As a result there was a certain strident patriotism, a feeling that the war was only just over, and this manifested itself in thousands of Union Jacks of all sizes, photographs of Churchill in most pubs and shop windows, and hundreds of posters showing a bulldog with a swastika between its teeth. The effect of this somewhat ostentatious Anglophilia was undermined by a small boy who approached us as we walked into St Peters Port and told us that he hated the British in general and British sailors in particular, a point he proceeded to amplify with a series of ineffectual but undoubtedly viciously intended kicks and blows.

It was a Sunday and the pubs were officially shut, but we were told that there was one open on the other side of the island. We found a café serving eggs in any quantity (there was still a severe shortage on the mainland), and I ate eight at a sitting cooked in many different ways, boiled, fried, poached and scrambled. I was to pay for this later with an angry boil on my leg. Towards evening we caught a bus in search of the pub. Felix was worrying about his sex-life, attributing his lack of success to his inability to distinguish between girls that might and those that wouldn't. Whenever we passed one he would ask us crossly 'Would she?' or 'What about her?' Edward Wood and I answered with an assumption of libidinous expertise to which we had no right.

The island seemed dull, even on so beautiful an evening. It was flat and littered with greenhouses, and, while there were many rather pretty Jersey cows, Felix told me, whether seriously or not I have never been able to decide, that they were 'un-fashionably light in colour'. We found the pub, a Thirties half-timbered building with those dispiriting horse-brasses in the saloon bar. It was quite lively however and half the ship's company had homed in on it. After a time Felix went off, with the gloomy air of one who foresees failure, to try and pick up a girl 'who might', but Edward and I stayed put and began to get drunk. As usual the beer acted as a catalyst. There was a faded blonde at the bar asking, from time to time, for a gin and tonic in a painfully refined accent. I said something about the Palladium to Edward and she intervened.

'Aye have sung there,' she told us. 'Aye have sung all over the West End in the old days. The Albert Hall, everywhere.'

She pointed to a variety bill for the local Palace that was pinned up behind the bar. At the bottom in very small letters it said 'Grace Roberts – the Welsh Nightingale'.

'The billing is all wrong,' she said. 'It is meant to include "of wireless, film, and television fame".'

This last surprised me particularly. There had been a little television before the war in London; my father had seen it once and thought there was no future in it, but it had hardly got going again by 1947.

There was a curious noise like a bullfrog. We turned to face a tiny shrivelled man in spectacles who smiled at us, opened his mouth and croaked again even more loudly. I thought he was suffering from some affliction and tried not to smile but when he had croaked twice more I realized he was doing it deliberately. He too pointed to the variety bill and I worked out that he must be 'Mimco – the Australian Mimic'. He treated us to quite a repertoire of imitations, but refused to perform his speciality – someone blowing up a bicycle tyre – on the grounds that it was too noisy.

Another figure, 'the Great Marvo', the top of the bill, executed several conjuring tricks. He had an enormous wart on the side of his nose, but his tricks were extremely boring. We fell into conversation with a separate group who turned out to be a rival concern, the local rep. They were rather pathetic and swanky and being unable to imitate bullfrogs or tell us what card we were holding, launched into elaborate dirty jokes involving a great many 'funny voices' and offered us free tickets to their next production, *Jane Eyre*, which, with that irritating habit actors have of shortening the names of plays (i.e. 'As you', 'Much' or 'The Dream'), they referred to as 'Jane'. They did, however, give us a lift back in their taxi to St Peters Port where Edward, who had a weak head, was sick over the seafront.

The next day I had no shore leave but one of my nautical-artistic duties to perform. Everywhere we went it was the custom of the *Dido* to hold a children's party and it was my job to make-up the boy seamen as 'pirates', a task I enjoyed possibly overmuch. Later I was on cell duties. Taff had been recaptured for about the fourth time and was behind bars until there was a chance to hand him over to the naval police for yet another spell in the glass-house. Despite the horrors to come, he seemed as cheerful as ever.

'They'll 'ave to dismiss me from the service sooner or later,' he said in his Cardiff accent. 'Stands to reason, Boyo.'

169

We were two days on the way to Chatham, the sea broken only by the ship's bows. Gazing over the side of the steady stream of foaming water rushing past the great metal plating, it was possible to believe that it was the ship which was static, the ocean on the move. On the deck, in the hallucinatory clarity of the summer light, two marines, wearing masks, fenced among the stanchards and bollards. Smoking a cigar, contemplating a pleasurable shit, I was visited by the temptation to sign on, to travel the world, to know that whatsoever happened I would be clothed, housed and fed. I rejected it almost immediately: the discipline, the monotony of the mess deck, the ship lying, a dispossessed hulk of rusting metal, in the dockyard drizzle. Besides, I had to admit, the Navy might well refuse to have me. Useless at all but the most menial tasks, both rebellious and, argumentative, I was more or less tolerated in the comparatively anarchic gap between war and peace; and while on the subject of Anarchism, it would be impossible to square up my convictions with a career in the Navy. As an infiltrator or saboteur? Not me. Anarchism was too noble a concept to be denied in this way. Its means must be as honourable as its ends. I was an open Anarchist, making no secret of my commitment to anyone who was prepared to listen. In my locker were neat piles of pamphlets by Bakunin, Kropotkin, George Woodcock and Herbert Read which I left systematically about the mess deck hoping someone might pick them up and become interested. Somebody had. Warrant Officer Perkins had picked them up and become very interested indeed.

Chapter 14

There was something afoot. The cancellation of the Scandinavian cruise, the unexpected return to Chatham, were more than just an Admiralty whim. Rumour ran riot, but we were not kept in the dark for long. The morning following our arrival both watches, including watch-keepers, were ordered to fall in on the quarterdeck – an unprecedented command in my experience. We were, the Commander told us, about to be addressed by the Captain, who had some very sad information to impart.

The Captain was a short, plump man, neither popular nor unpopular, and indeed seldom seen by anyone below decks except for the wardroom stewards and the ratings on the bridge. He told us first that he would shortly be leaving the ship, probably during the Scottish voyage, and that the Commander would be assuming temporary command. If this had been all he had to tell us, we would have felt that, in implying that it was enough to reduce the ship's company to manly tears, the Commander had misinterpreted our feelings towards his rather anonymous superior officer. It was however only coincidental. The reason why the Captain was leaving the ship was because the Admiralty had decided ('Whether rightly or wrongly,' said the Captain in a rare display of feeling), that the *Dido* was for the scrap-heap, redundant! This, he added, would not of course affect those due for demob, but he was sure it would be a matter of regret for the regular ship's company, who would shortly have to return to their barracks for re-posting. Meanwhile he hoped that the spirit of the ship . . .

Where he was wrong, in my case at any rate, was in believing that only the regular ship's company would be upset. I am by nature sentimental to a fault, and it was all I could do not to sob audibly. It was ironic that the very next day I was to be put on a serious charge which could have given me cause to cry in earnest.

That evening, too short of funds and too despondent to go 'up the smoke', Felix, Edward and I, all of us due for demob in a few weeks, got maudlin drunk, on the *Dido*'s behalf, in a gloomy Chatham pub. The beer was responsible for a minor disaster that night. In a dockyard they lock up the 'heads' to avoid polluting the harbour and any rating taken short is expected to go ashore and use the latrines on the quay. Sensibly enough nobody does. An empty tickler tin is left by the open porthole, and is baled out into the darkness as many times as it is filled. Rising crossly from my hammock I grabbed the tickler tin and began peeing in it, only to find that despite aiming accurately (a fact I checked) I was soaking my feet. In my fuddled state it took me some time to work out why. An empty tickler tin can be put to several uses, and one of them is for helping to make the washing-up water soapy. To do this all that's necessary is to punch several holes in the bottom, put in some fragments of issue soap and then swish the tin rapidly around in the hot water until it produces sufficient lather. In my haste to relieve myself I had grabbed the wrong tin. Lying in my hammock with damp feet, I began to feel a little less sentimental about the *Dido*.

The next day Warrant Officer Perkins approached me with a

look of grim satisfaction on his face. I was to come up to the locker flat and open my locker. Why, I wondered? He surely couldn't have persuaded the Commander that Le Viol was obscene after all. The Commander was waiting there looking rather severe. I smiled at him and he didn't smile back, but asked me to open it up. I did so. Warrant Officer Perkins pointed to the Freedom Press pamphlets. The Commander asked me what they were and why I had so many of each. I told him that they were Anarchist literature and whenever possible I distributed them among the sailors. A look of total astonishment passed across the Commander's kindly aquiline features. Did I realize that these were subversive pamphlets aimed at undermining the State, the Armed Forces, the Church, even the Navy itself? I said yes of course I did, but . . .

There was no but. I was on Commander's defaulters next day and had better recognize the seriousness of the charge. If proven it could lead to a court martial. Shore leave suspended. Warrant Officer Perkins took the pamphlets, but I asked for an example of each to prepare my defence. The Commander nodded. I took them and went aloft, rather perplexed, to talk to Felix.

Felix was not perplexed at all. Anarchism opposed, both in general and in detail, the whole structure of society from the Head of State down. It was quite specific in declaring that its triumph could only be achieved through revolution. It dismissed all armed forces as the tools of the status quo and elective representation as a sham. I pointed out that so did Bernard Shaw, and yet there was a complete edition of his plays and prefaces in the ship's library. A good point, Felix conceded, and his advice to me was to spend the evening marking suitable passages on such subjects as Royalty, God, the military, politicians and anything else relevant in support of my case. I did what he suggested, and, before slinging my hammock, had found a selection of quotes which, taken out of context, made the Anarchist pamphlets sound understated.

Next day I faced the Commander. Perkins made a statement; finding a tract on the table in F mess, reading it and discovering it to be not only subversive but, and here he coloured, an attack on

God, the King and every other institution and standard that decent ordinary people held sacred . . . There was a great deal of feeling and passion in Warrant Officer Perkins. His animosity was not entirely personal. He genuinely loathed everything I subscribed to. The Commander asked me what I had to say. I began by asserting (here again Felix had advised me) that if the recent war stood for anything, it was to ensure freedom of thought and expression to all, including those holding minority views – even those which might appear repulsive to many people. The Commander made vaguely sympathetic noises to all this; Warrant Officer Perkins clearly dismissed it as immaterial. After a short pause the Commander became more specific, opening what he called 'this twopenny-halfpenny subversive rubbish' and asking me, as a member of the armed forces, to justify its dissemination. He then read out certain passages and I retaliated with one of my prepared quotes from Shaw. To begin with he asked if this was relevant. I assured him it was so, and he accepted it. Warrant Officer Perkins made it clear in his cold way that if he were sitting in judgment he'd have thrown the collected works of the Sage of Ayot St Lawrence into the harbour. After we'd covered Royalty, God, the family, universal suffrage, the profession of arms and kindred topics – the Commander reading from the Anarchists in measured tones, me trying to make Shaw sound as inflammatory as possible – he asked me what formed the basis of my quote-for-quote defence. I, in return, asked him if he found the passages from Shaw as subversive as those from Kropotkin, Woodcock and other libertarians. He admitted he did so. I then pointed out that I had borrowed the collected works of Shaw from the ship's library, where they were freely available to the entire ship's company.

The Commander paused. A very slight smile hovered about his face. He suppressed it. Shaw, he said, was after all a famous writer. These chaps, and he gestured dismissively at the pamphlets, well he'd never even heard of them. That was an easy one. In that case Shaw was the more dangerous. A famous writer must surely carry more weight than the authors of 'twopenny-halfpenny pamphlets'.

This was of course untrue and I knew it. Famous writers in general, and Shaw in particular, are licensed. For those seeking a voice to speak up for them, a prophet to translate their discontent into issues and actions, the eloquent unknown subversive carries far more weight than a famous jester of the Establishment. This happily didn't occur to the Commander. He remained silent for some time. Then he gave judgment: I was an educated man. Much as he disapproved of them, it was possible for me to read and even benefit from such writings. The majority of the Lower Deck was not so privileged and might take everything literally. It could be especially dangerous for those who had made the Navy their career. As I was due for demob in a few weeks, he had decided not to proceed with the charge. I daren't look at Warrant Officer Perkins. Any sign from me of triumph or satisfaction might have driven him over the edge. The Commander continued: he was confiscating all my Anarchist literature. It would be returned to my home address after my demobilization. He understood from Warrant Officer Perkins that I also subscribed to an Anarchist newspaper. I must cancel this or have it sent home. Anything to say?

'Thank you, sir.'

'That's all right, Melly, but any further infringement of my ruling and you'll be on a very serious charge indeed. Case dismissed.'

'About turn,' shouted the Chief Petty Officer. 'Quick march,' and, into my ear, 'Jammy bastard!'

I'd won! Warrant Officer Perkins had lost his last and most serious bid to undo me. I told Felix that I'd triumphed entirely through his advice and my own eloquence, and I believed it. It seems to me now that the fact the Commander quite liked me and was perfectly well aware that Warrant Officer Perkins had it in for me were equally valid reasons for his decision, and that the knowledge that I'd only a few weeks to go in the service and the sweat involved in setting up a court martial may well have come into it too.

Although I didn't connect the two things at the time, I'm now convinced that my non-appearance at the Royal Naval Command variety performance two weeks later was the work of the Warrant Officer. The chaplain told me the powers that be had decided my act wasn't suitable after all, and the other *Dido* entrant, a writer called Chinnery, a rather humdrum amateur conjuror of the 'take a card' school, appeared instead. I was upset but never for a moment thought that my defence of Anarchism had anything to do with disqualifying me from singing 'Frankie and Johnny' in front of the King.

Freed from the Commander's ban on shore leave I went up to London a couple of times but found it less satisfactory and stimulating than during my distant days on the *Argus*. Many of the people I rang up were either away or engaged or said they were. I'd told most of them I was coming to live and work there after my demob and the prospect of being used as a convenient and regular source of food and drink by a penniless art gallery assistant was obviously less attractive than an occasional visit from a bellbottomed sailor.

The Mesens, of course, were a different matter, but here things were if anything less satisfactory. The gallery was almost ready to open: the coconut matting was down, the bookshelves installed and above the desk behind which I was to sit, a high relief sculpture by F. E. McWilliam of a vast displaced eye, ear, nose and mouth was already in position. What I found worrying was Edouard's excessively businesslike approach. He dismissed my highly coloured version of my pro-Anarchist stand rather impatiently, concentrating almost entirely on my future duties – the till, the addressing of invitation cards, the telephone switch-board, the invoicing of accounts – and he told me that I must go to nightschool to learn French. He also let out that he had written to my parents suggesting that, after I'd left the Navy, I should return home for three months to master touch-typing and short-hand. Writing to my parents behind my back! Was this the act of a Surrealist poet?

The Surrealist Group had almost entirely disintegrated. Most of the foreigners had returned home and Simon, who had anyway quarrelled again with E.L.T., had joined BOAC as a steward. Sadi Cherkeshi had gone to train as a naval architect in Istanbul.

I visited his ex-landlord, the gruff and humorous W. S. Meadmore of Margaretta Terrace, S.W.3, and he, at least, I found totally unchanged. His wife still took lodgers and, although they were full at the moment, it occurred to me that, nearer the time of my coming to live in London, I might write and ask him if they would be prepared to take me on. Meadmore apart, I returned to Chatham wondering if I wouldn't have preferred the life of a cub-reporter on a Liverpool paper after all.

We left for Scotland which, like Guernsey, I resented as not being 'really abroad'. After four days at sea we anchored at Rosyth. Felix and I went once to Edinburgh, a city with which I fell instantly in love. It was not so much the old town, despite its twisting, rather sinister medieval juxtaposition of squalor and grandeur and its association with Burke and Hare, which attracted me, nor yet the austere beauty of the Georgian new town. It was the rich absurdity of the Scottish Victoriana.

We dined in what was then called the Caledonian Snack Bar and is now the downstairs bar of the Café Royal but is otherwise mercifully unchanged. Behind the carved mahogany bar several magnificent stained-glass windows of sportsmen in the fashions of the 1870s: a cricketer with his beard and bat, a football player, a fisherman, a clean-shaven huntsman, a bewhiskered deer-stalker. The evening light, streaming through these worthies, cast lozenges of purple and red light on our lobster and schooners of sherry. On the walls were ceramic tiled murals of famous nineteenth-century inventors and scientists.

We steamed up to Nairn, a grey little town where it was drizzling, and Felix thought the moment had come to produce a bottle of Schnapps he'd smuggled aboard at Frederikshaven. Edward had bought a little guidebook and, as the level of the Schnapps went down, it drove us into increasingly manic hysterics. 'Nairn folk,' it read 'look at you with kind eyes, schoolchildren smile and give you a cheery "hello" and babies in their prams wave fat little hands at you.'

The next day, the three of us walked to look at Cawdor Castle, an expedition that for some reason brought my insane and confused bouillabaisse of snobbery to the boil. 'It has that indefinable feeling of history, of a line of sperm, of continuous possession which no public park of National Trust property can have,' I told Felix. To ease my Anarchist conscience at these crypto-Fascist notions, I added that the only way to defeat 'the aristocratic seduction' was 'a general aristocracy of the spirit'. 'Man,' I told him and Edward, 'must possess the nobility of the lion, the grace of the antelope, the lust of the goat. It is no solution to tear down castles in order to erect grey housing estates or pessary factories.'

Acting on permission from the lodge-keeper, we wandered about the grounds and were rewarded by the sight of the seven-year-old young Laird playing with his nursemaid. 'Fair-haired and sturdy' was how I described him, and I was delighted when he waved to us from his nursery window as we were leaving.

On the walk back to Nairn, I launched into praise of the pre-Raphaelites. Not of course 'their deplorable religious works', but their veneration for 'the details of a hedgerow, the intricate veining of leaves, the furry underside of nettles, the berries, grasses and bright-eyed birds'. How Edward and Felix let me get away with it speaks more for their tolerance than my oratory, still less my ideology. I do remember thinking that Edward seemed 'rather silent' but put this down of course to his 'dislike of walking'.

That evening in Nairn we went to the cinema to see that excellent American thriller *The Lady in The Lake*, but here too I couldn't resist drawing conclusions afterwards. If the film was accurate, to fight in the defence of 'the American way of life' was absurd. Negroes, bums, outcasts, and rebels were the true heroes of the USA . . . Unlike my earlier eulogy for 'the line of sperm', it was at least a view which would have found favour in the decades to come, but it was just as glib, just as unconnected with any evaluation based on experience. Waiting on the jetty – the water still and milky, the sky primrose yellow, the ship twinkling half a mile out – I finally shut up. A Cornish Able Seaman we all knew slightly and who, sober, had struck us as a rather dour figure behind his formidable black beard, was trying to persuade his equally drunk friend that no good would come of his attempt to approach, with bestial intentions, a small white dog sitting under the marble statue of a Victorian divine holding a bible.

'Moi old lady,' he said, 'as gart six black cats. They be better for 'un than thart gude darg!'

He kept it up in the liberty boat. After observing the *Dido*'s Medical Officer and schoolmaster, who had been ashore together and were both very pissed, he concluded that, 'the doc's after the schoolie's arse, but the schoolie's so drunk and wet 'e don't know whart e's up to'. We could see no basis for this observation but found it amusing enough nevertheless. 'Besoides,' he added as an afterthought, 'Doc's so drunk 'eself 'e couldn't roightly tell if oi 'ad sif or crabs.'

We laughed a lot, while behind us the darkness obscured 'the furry undersides of nettles' and 'the bright-eyed birds', and the reels of film proving 'the absurdity of fighting for the American way of life' lay stacked in the projection room of the Nairn Electric Kinema.

'Who'll give me his tot if I tell them where they can find a sheep and lend them my seaboots?' It was the Baron who made this offer as he stared through the porthole at Loch Ewe, a bleak stretch of water in the North-West Highlands surrounded by featureless hills on which, indeed, a few sheep grazed. Sheep-shagging in sparsely populated areas is a well-established naval myth and there was an apocryphal but much repeated story that at Scapa Flow during the war a rating accused of the practice told his Commander that he had mistaken the sheep for a WREN in a duffle coat.

We didn't go ashore as the weather was foul and there was nothing to do except walk, but this didn't stop me watching, with envious irritation, the First Lieutenant and the ship's doctor setting off with their rods, and later, feeling equally put out to find five or six freckled brown trout lying on a large white dish in the wardroom when I and the Marine Corporal were carrying out one of our raids on the wardroom galley during the middle watch. I had not fished since before the war, and was not to do so again until the middle Fifties, but, like those diseases which lie dormant for several years only to break out with renewed vigour, I was still a fisherman waiting only for the opportunity to start again.

We had joined up with the *Superb*, the *Cleopatra*, the *Diadem* and the *Syrius* in order to paint ship for the royal inspection. The prospect was grim and, as always when boredom was unavoidable, frustration spread through the ship like a virus and tempers became frayed. Next day there was a fight. Our mess deck had just been painted prior to admiral's rounds when a Geordie sickberth attendant, who had been circulating round the ship claiming 'sippers' of rum to celebrate his birthday, staggered in. Now that rum is no longer issued in the Navy this could not happen but in those days it was the custom for any sailor who had a birthday to visit every mess claiming 'sippers' until such time as he collapsed. Admittedly this practice was officially forbidden ever since, according to legend, two popular identical twins, taking advantage of the tradition, were given so much that they both died of alcoholic poisoning, but it was still observed nevertheless. The Geordie was long past wanting any more rum anyway, he was simply on the way to his own mess to collapse, but he was so drunk that he pushed out of his path the duty cook who was dividing the currant duff. There were general cries of 'fuck off', but the Baron varied the formula by adding 'four eyes' to his directive and, as the sickberth attendant wore very strong pebble glasses, this penetrated his fuddled consciousness, and breaking into great sobs of rage he shouted out, 'Ah'll rip your bludy throut out Baron,' and flew at him. The Baron behaved with (for him) remarkable restraint ('Well, I couldn't go for a man half-canned,' he explained later) and the Geordie was pulled off him by members of both messes, but so great was his rum-fuelled rage that he broke loose and went for his opponent again and again. His shirt was in ribbons, his uniform covered in wet paint and dirt, his face filthy, tear-stained and horrifying in its impotent rage. I watched him with appalled fascination. Here was *l'homme moyen sensuel* with a vengeance! The climax came when, swinging round, he knocked a large tray of custard all over the newly painted hatch-combing. The Baron slid tactfully away and the boy, still shouting threats, allowed himself to be led off to his mess. When he came to several hours later he apologized to the Baron, who said, 'That's all right, mate.' This allowed me to theorize at tedious length to Felix on the merits of instant violence (working class) as opposed to the vice of storing up resentment and listing scores to be settled (bourgeois). The fact was I had been disturbed by the fight and needed to rationalize it in order to find it acceptable.

While the painting was going on we had a small ship's concert on board and Felix and I wrote a sketch for it full of cracks about the various officers. Edward, Felix, John the homosexual writer and I acted in it, and it went down very well. Later that evening, just as I was turning in, a wardroom steward came into the mess and asked me if we could do it again for the officers as they were giving a farewell dinner for the Captain and one of the Lieutenants, who'd been at the concert, thought it might amuse him. It was well if noisily received and we were given a lot of gin afterwards, although this time I was careful to avoid excess and got back to my hammock without delivering a revolutionary diatribe or being sick over anyone's shoes. Next morning the ship, a smart grey from bow to stern, steamed slowly out of Loch Ewe, perhaps to the relief of the sheep, and headed south towards the Clyde.

This, had I still been performing in the Royal Command concert, would have been a time of mounting excitement. As it was I felt pretty sour about the whole thing. On arrival we took up our position, ships of all sizes as far as the eye could see. A useless congress of metal, I thought to myself. 'A magnificent spectacle,' said the commentator over the mess radio. The bullshit was intensified hourly. 'No overalls on the upper deck,' barked the tannoy. 'Collars will be worn until 2000 hours.'

The arrival of the Royal Family sent the press and wireless into that curious state of mind where any sign of normal behaviour on their part was described as if it were a charming form of eccentricity. 'The Queen smiled at Princess Margaret, who ran back to the car to fetch her shoes. She smiled and said "thank you",' explained the *Daily Express*. 'A delightful homely moment there,' said the radio commentator. 'Princess Elizabeth has leant forward and made some adjustment to her mother's veil.'

The inspection went smoothly enough. Three cheers, the guns booming, and a distant glimpse of royalty.

'If the government is preparing for another war,' I asked Felix, 'why aren't we on intensive training? On the other hand, if we're as broke as they tell us, why are we spending money on treating the Navy as an expensive toy for gawping crowds, and a means of livelihood for sparrow-brained radio announcers?'

Edward Wood said, 'You can't dislike the Royal Family. You can only feel sorry for them.'

That evening writer Chinnery performed his royal conjuring tricks and I got sullenly drunk in Glasgow.

We hung about the Clyde for a few days before heading down the west coast – the *Dido* for the knacker's yard and me for demob.

The ship's company was dwindling. The Captain was piped ashore and, later the same day, the Baron left us. His exit was typical, standing on the quay in the pouring rain without an oilskin, shouting obscenities and clutching the recordings of his beloved Johann Sebastian. I never saw or heard of him again.

We reached Chatham on 8 August and, as there was a bottle-neck in the demobilization programme, I was sent home on a fortnight's leave. This meant that I had my twenty-first birthday in Liverpool and I asked Felix and Edward up to celebrate. My father photographed us, surrounded by uncles, aunts and cousins, on the lawn. It was a time of limbo.

I returned, not to the ship but to barracks, and another three weeks passed. I didn't go ashore. I felt a curious numbing apathy, expecting every day to be sent for and handed my railway warrant to York, where there was a depot for civilian clothing. I was given useless but easy jobs. I felt a sentimental regret for the end of the *Dido*, and even for my release from the Navy itself.

One fine September morning I was sweeping the barrack paths with an elderly Leading Seaman. I was wondering how, without offending him, I could avoid the proposition he was working up to – 'I'd sooner 'ave a naughty boy than a naughty girl,' he told me by way of a preliminary come-on – when I saw, hurrying along between the neat flower beds and painted ship's figureheads, the same agitated White-Rabbit-like Lieutenant who had sent me to the *Dido* over a year before. He told me I should have been demobbed two weeks earlier and seemed to suggest it was somehow my fault. With some relief I said goodbye to the old salt and followed the Lieutenant to his office. Two hours later I was on my way to York.

In the warehouse I chose a brown herring-bone suit, two shirts, a striped tie, four pairs of socks, four pairs of pants and vests, shoes and a fawn mac. There were also a pair of cuff links, back and front studs, and two collars. These were packed in a box; we had to travel home in our uniforms, and we were warned that if, in the street outside, we were offered six pounds for our civvies we were to refuse, as they were worth at least twice that much.

Nobody offered me six pounds. I walked to the station. It was almost exactly three years to the day since I'd left Liverpool for Skegness. What had I learnt? How to pipe a Captain on board. How to make rope-ends 'tiddly' on deck. How to wank in a hammock without waking up the entire mess. It was time to leave the navy-blue womb, the steel-clad egg. Full of confused but passionately-held theories, and unjustified confidence in my ability to win through instantly, I caught the train home. There was a neat parcel waiting for me stamped OHMS. It contained the Anarchist pamphlets.